BATTLE OF THE AISNE

13th–15th SEPTEMBER, 1914

TOUR OF THE BATTLEFIELD

The Naval & Military Press Ltd

Published by
The Naval & Military Press Ltd
Unit 10 Ridgewood Industrial Park,
Uckfield, East Sussex,
TN22 5QE England
Tel: +44 (0) 1825 749494
Fax: +44 (0) 1825 765701
www.naval-military-press.com

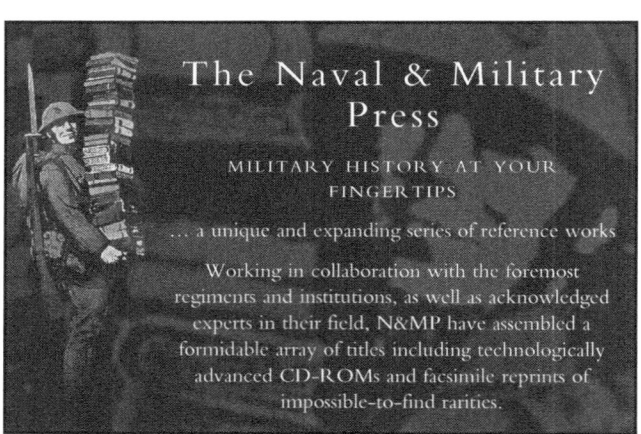

In reprinting in facsimile from the original, any imperfections are inevitably reproduced and the quality may fall short of modern type and cartographic standards.

OFFICIAL COPY.

Notified in Army Orders for December, 1934

26
Publications
3199

BATTLE OF THE AISNE

13th–15th SEPTEMBER, 1914

TOUR OF THE BATTLEFIELD

By Command of the Army Council,

THE WAR OFFICE,
31st *December,* 1934

57-501-0-34

THE information given in this pamphlet is intended to form a *framework* only for the study by officers of the Official History and other books dealing with the Battle of the Aisne (1914) and the events leading up to that battle.

CONTENTS

	PAGE
I.—Events leading up to the Battle of the Aisne	5
II.—Notes on the 1914 training manuals	9
III.—Summary of the battle 12th–15th September	13
IV.—Tour of the battlefield with incidents in the battle	17
V.—Principal lessons of the battle	38
VI.—The unconquerable mind. A study of a night operation	42
VII.—Retrospect of the battle	47
VIII.—Order of battle of troops engaged—	
(a) British	49
(b) French	53
(c) German	53
IX.—Legend.—For use with tracing of dispositions of British and German artillery on 14th September	55

In pocket at end of pamphlet

Map 1.—Advance of the B.E.F. on 12th and 13th September.

Map 2.—Situation at nightfall, 14th September.

Map 3.—The AISNE battlefield, 1914.

Sketch 4.—Diagram to illustrate difficulties of British artillery.

Sketch 5.—Panorama from spur north of CONDE about 815900 looking east.

Sketch 6.—Panorama from CHIVRES spur about 802886 looking south-west.

Sketch 7.—Sketch map and panorama to illustrate the attack of 1 Div. on TROYON, 14th September.

Sketch 8.—Tracing to fit over Map 2 showing dispositions of British and German artillery on 14th September.

I

SUMMARY OF EVENTS LEADING UP TO THE BATTLE OF THE AISNE

1. 27th August–3rd September. The retreat.

In accordance with the original German plan, after the battle of LE CATEAU (26 Aug.) the German First (Von Kluck) and Second (Von Bülow) Armies, both under the general direction of Von Bülow, continued their march, Von Kluck towards the Lower SEINE, west of PARIS, and Von Bülow direct on PARIS. These orders were confirmed by O.H.L.* on 28 Aug. The general direction was thus south-west, whilst the B.E.F. and French Fifth Army (Lanrezac) retired in a rather more southerly direction. With the exception of a halt for rest on 29 Aug., the B.E.F. continued the retreat day by day without incident apart from rear guard and outpost actions of more or less local importance. The B.E.F. did not again come into action as a whole until the advance to the MARNE began on 6 Sep.

Meanwhile, on 29 Aug., Lanrezac's Fifth Army attacked Von Bülow's Second Army in the vicinity of GUISE, and obtained in the two days' fighting some measure of success on its right flank and generally checking, if only temporarily, the advance of Von Bülow's Army.

On 30th, Von Kluck, who had been released from Von Bülow's control on 27th, without orders from Von Moltke and in response to a request from Von Bülow, turned south-east with a view to finishing off the French Fifth Army. He thus missed the chance of enveloping Maunoury's Sixth Army, which was in process of formation north of PARIS on the left of the B.E.F. This change of direction was approved by O.H.L. on the 31st.

On 31st, Von Kluck's two leading corps (IX and III) crossed the OISE north of COMPIEGNE and advanced about 12 miles beyond the river, while his rear corps (IV Res.) was in and south of AMIENS. Von Kluck was now moving south-eastwards north of the AISNE, while the B.E.F. was marching more or less south-westwards on the other side of the river.

On 1 Sep., Von Kluck, finding the B.E.F. on his right flank, gave up his advance against the French Fifth Army and turned south in an effort to settle with the B.E.F. Rear guard engagements took place at NERY, CREPY-EN-VALOIS and VILLERS COTTERETS.

---

*NOTE.—"O.H.L.," stands for "Oberste Heeresleitung," *i.e.*, Supreme Command.

On 2 Sep., Von Kluck again advanced against the B.E.F. but, finding about midday that it had slipped away, wheeled his two eastern corps (IX and III) south-east against the flank of the French Fifth Army, while the remainder continued the advance on PARIS. Von Bülow had now reached the AISNE between PONTAVERT and SOISSONS whilst Lanrezac had fallen back to the line REIMS—FERE-EN-TARDENOIS.

Meanwhile, on 1 Sep., Sir John French had made a proposal to the French Minister of War to organize a line of defence on the MARNE and there to stand against the attack of the enemy. This was rejected next day by Joffre, who considered that the co-operation of the B.E.F. in the defence of PARIS would afford " un resultat avantageux." The same evening orders were issued by Joffre for a general retirement, the limit of which was to be behind the SEINE, the AUBE and the ORNAIN.

On the night of 2/3 Sep., O.H.L. issued orders to Von Kluck and Von Bülow that the French were to be forced away from PARIS in a south-easterly direction, and that Von Kluck was to follow in echelon behind Von Bülow and to be responsible for the flank protection of the force. Von Kluck accordingly detailed the IV Res. Corps and a cavalry division for the flank protection against PARIS and, disregarding the letter of his orders whilst carrying out their spirit, pushed on and crossed the MARNE against the French, keeping the II Corps in echelon behind his right as a further protection against PARIS.

2. The counter offensive.

Up to this moment O.H.L. was under the impression that all was going well, but on the evening of 4 Sep. realized that the attempt to envelop the Allies had failed and issued orders as follows :—

Von Kluck and Von Bülow to face the east front of PARIS between the OISE and the SEINE. The Fourth (Duke Albrecht) and Fifth (Crown Prince) Armies to continue the advance south-eastwards in accordance with the original plan and endeavour to facilitate the passage of the Sixth (Prince Rupprecht) and Seventh (Von Heeringen) Armies across the MOSELLE.

The Third (Von Hausen) Army to co-operate with Von Bülow on its right or Duke Albrecht on its left as the situation demanded.

A primarily defensive role was thus imposed on Von Kluck and Von Bülow.

As the orders were received too late for Von Kluck to countermand the marches ordered for 5th, by the evening of that day four of his corps (IX, III, IV and II) with two cavalry divisions ahead were along the GRAND MORIN with a flank guard of one corps (IV Res.) and one cavalry division north of the MARNE some 20 miles in rear facing west. At this time the B.E.F. was halted for the night on the general line ROZOY—TOURNAN—OZOIR-LA-FERRIERE, S.S.E. of PARIS.

Von Kluck in his impetuosity had now exposed himself to attack on his right flank by both Maunoury and the B.E.F.

On the morning of 4th and on 5th, Joffre issued orders for the offensive. Those issued on 4th, which concerned the B.E.F., did not, however, reach G.H.Q. until the morning of 5th.

The general plan was as follows :—

On the east, the Third (Sarrail) Army was to attack westwards (from the vicinity of VERDUN). On the west, the Sixth (Maunoury) Army, the B.E.F., and the Fifth (Franchet d'Esperey)* Army, were to attack generally eastwards, while the Ninth (Foch) and Fourth (Langle de Cary) Armies in the centre were to hold up the German advance on their fronts.

Unfortunately, owing to a chapter of accidents, the B.E.F. had during 5th, continued the retreat for a further 12 miles beyond the position (viz., CHANGIS—COULOMMIERS) on which Joffre had based his plan and orders.

On 5th, Maunoury moved forward, and in the afternoon two of his reserve divisions fought an action with the German IV Res. Corps, the only portion of Von Kluck's Army, except the 4th Cavalry Division, north of the MARNE. The Germans were completely surprised, and were more so still next day when the general attack was launched. Von Kuhl (Von Kluck's Chief of Staff) writes " No sign, no prisoner's statement, no newspaper paragraph gave us warning of it." During the night of 5/6 Sep., Von Kluck ordered the two corps (II and IV) which were in front of the British to counter-march at 5 a.m. next day and hustle to the help of the IV Res. Corps, north of the MARNE. He left his remaining two corps (III and IX) behind, handing them over temporarily to Von Bülow. Thus a gap was formed between the right of the Second Army about COURTACON and the left of the First Army on the MARNE, which was filled by Von der Marwitz's and Von Richthofen's Cavalry Corps together with some weak infantry rear guards.

On 6th, the attack started in accordance with Joffre's orders. The B.E.F., after some skirmishing with the cavalry and rear guards, by evening gained the line of the GRAND MORIN ; on its right the French Fifth Army made steady progress during the day, whilst on its left Maunoury, who brought up his strength chiefly on the north, that is his left, made progress after heavy fighting in that quarter. Further east the Ninth and Fourth Armies were heavily attacked and forced to give ground slightly, while the attack of the Third Army failed.

---

* NOTE.—Franchet d'Esperey had relieved Lanrezac in command of the Fifth French Army on 3 Sep.

On 7th, Maunoury was reinforced by the IV Corps which had detrained in PARIS, and Von Kluck, seeing the danger of the situation, in the morning asked, Von Bülow for help, claiming the two corps, which he had handed over to him the day before, and asking at the same time that they should be directed towards his right about LA FERTE MILON and CROUY. When these two corps had left, Von Bülow's right flank about MONTMIRAIL was unprotected, and a gap of some 25 miles, covered only by cavalry and cyclists, was left between the First and Second Armies. Into this gap the B.E.F. advanced, crossing the PETIT MORIN on 8th and the MARNE on 9th, whilst the left corps of the French Fifth Army drove back Von Bülow's right. At the same time west of the MARNE, Von Kluck, who was now in superior strength to Maunoury, having turned the latter's left flank, was within reasonable measure of victory. The situation on the western half of the battle front had thus become very interesting.

3. The German retreat.

On the evening of 8th, Colonel Von Hentsch, who had been sent out by O.H.L. to co-ordinate the retreat of the German armies on the west "should rearward movements have already been initiated," arrived at Von Bülow's H.Q. He left these H.Q. in the early morning of 9th, after Von Bülow had decided to order the withdrawal of his Army, which began soon after midday. On arrival at Von Kluck's H.Q. about 1 p.m., Von Hentsch, in virtue of the powers conferred on him by O.H.L., ordered the withdrawal of the First Army.

Of the fighting on the remainder of the front there is little of importance to recount. All along the line little progress could be made by the French against the attacks and counter-attacks of Duke Albrecht's and Von Hausen's Armies.

On 10 Sep., Von Kluck was once again placed under the orders of Von Bülow, who at the same time was ordered by O.H.L. to retire behind the VESLE. The Third and Fourth Armies were ordered to retire behind the AISNE.

On 10th and 11th, the B.E.F. and the French Fifth and Sixth Armies followed up and many prisoners were taken. By that evening, Von Kluck had withdrawn to the AISNE between SOISSONS on the east and ATTICHY on the west.

As the result of the fighting on the western flank of the battle line, the German sweep through Belgium and France was stopped. The enemy was forced to give ground and evacuate French territory over which they had only just advanced. The German plan had failed and with it all chance of an immediate victory had vanished. The Allies had been given breathing time.

II

NOTES ON THE 1914 TRAINING MANUALS

1. Advanced guards and pursuit.

Field Service Regulations, Part I, 1909, did not differ greatly from the present-day manuals as regards general principles.

The need for a vigorous offensive is emphasized and in particular the importance of the time factor. " A commander who has gained a strategical advantage may have to act at once in order to prevent the enemy bringing about conditions more favourable to himself " (Sec. 99, 3).

The necessity of allowing the enemy no respite in pursuit was fully realized. It was " to continue by day and night without regard to the exhaustion of men and horses." And again, " All pursuing troops should act with the greatest boldness and be prepared to accept risks which would not be justifiable at other times " (Sec. 112). In point of fact the advance on 12 Sep. was most cautious, and the affair at BRAINE delayed the march for three hours.

The employment of mounted troops " to seize and hold positions in front of the slower moving infantry " was envisaged, and in particular defiles and bridges are referred to.

In 1914, the underlying theory as regards the employment of artillery with the advanced guard was to deceive the enemy as to the number of guns actually available to support the advanced guard. Wide dispersion and liberal expenditure of ammunition was recommended. Today artillery is recognized as the main weapon to assist the advanced guard to maintain its progress.

2. Deployment for action.

The teaching of 1914 was for troops to maintain their march formations until a plan had been made and, though units were to close up before deploying, " when time presses it may be necessary to move units directly from the line of march into their position in the deployed line, but this is likely to result in the troops being employed piecemeal " (F.S.R., Part I, 1909, Sec. 102, 2). This is exactly what did happen (*see* Stand No. 7—Operations of 1 Div. on 14 Sep.). The tendency of the present day is to adopt preparatory formations earlier, *see* F.R.S., Vol. II, 1929, Sec. 26, 2.

In the same section of the 1909 regulations in heavy type we find :—

" The first object of a commander who seeks to gain the initiative in battle is to develop superiority of fire as a preparation for the delivery of a decisive blow."

3. The attack—General.

"The general principle is that the enemy must be engaged in sufficient strength to pin him to his ground—while the force allotted to the decisive attack must be as strong as possible." The force necessary for such an operation was decided almost entirely on man power per yard of front. "The latest experience goes to show that a smaller force than from three to five men per yard on the front on which the decisive attack is to be delivered will rarely prove sufficient, this force being distributed in such depth as circumstances make advisable" (F.S.R., Part I, 1909, Sec. 104, 3). No mention of artillery is made except that "it should be so distributed as to be able to support the infantry when required." Rifle fire was the chief consideration at that period. Today frontages are considered in terms of ground and available fire power (F.S.R., Vol. II, 1929, Sec. 61, 3).

4. The conduct of the attack.

The attacking infantry was divided into a *firing line* a proportion of which was usually to be kept back as *supports*. Behind these followed *local reserves* in the hand of battalion, brigade and divisional commanders.

The firing line was to press forward at all costs and, when it came under effective fire, its further advance was to be assisted by covering fire by artillery, machine guns and special detachments of infantry. Mutual support in the firing line though regarded as desirable was expected to be more automatic than deliberately arranged. In the later stages of the attack the infantry was to advance by rushes; creeping and advancing man by man was discouraged. Thus a firing line was built up usually within close infantry range of the enemy and an infantry fire fight ensued, culminating, when the fire of the defenders slackened, in the assault.

The impetus for the assault was expected to come from the firing line on the initiative of the forward infantry commander; no time could therefore be fixed with the artillery, who had to co-operate as best they could.

No method of co-ordinating the operation of the various arms in a fire plan was envisaged in 1914. The importance of a carefully prepared fire plan to-day is due to the necessity for overcoming the stopping power of the machine gun, of which far greater numbers are available than in 1914, and the consequent increased power of the defence.

5. Artillery—General.

(a) In 1914, no centralized control of the artillery beyond the division was contemplated, and no higher artillery commanders or staffs, or C.B.Os., were in existence.

The 1914 regulations provided for decentralization, by the formation of groups of infantry and artillery within the division for distinct tactical operations (F.S.R., Part I, 1909, Sec. 105, 3), but the present day distinction between artillery "under command" and "in support" was not laid down.

(b) The importance of employing the maximum number of guns for vital tasks was not realized, probably owing to the absence of arrangements for control (*see* above).

"The number of batteries employed" (*e.g.*, to support the assault) "should be limited to the number which can be effectively controlled" (F.A.T., 1914, Sec. 157, 4).

(c) The 1914 regulations did not appreciate the value of concentrated artillery fire.

(d) The 1914 regulations stress the importance of maintaining a proportion of guns in reserve.

"As a general principle, fire should not be opened with more guns than are necessary to accomplish the task in hand, the remainder being kept in positions of readiness" (F.S.R., Part I, 1909, Sec. 105, 1).

The 1914 regulations did not regard artillery in action as forming a reserve of fire power and did not consider disposing artillery so as to be able to switch its fire to different portions of the front.

(e) The necessity for co-operation between infantry and artillery commanders was emphasized in the 1914 regulations, but the system of close liaison between artillery and infantry was not so highly developed as it is to-day.

(f) The spirit of the 1914 regulations tended to make batteries take up positions in the open, in order to give continuous support in the later stages of an attack, and this led to heavy losses on the AISNE.

On the AISNE, battery commanders certainly carried out their tasks to the full in the spirit of the 1914 regulations, but were handicapped by lack of higher direction.

(g) The 1914 regulations did not contemplate the use of F.O.Os. except in very exceptional circumstances, as batteries were expected to be pushed right forward to support the assault; the necessity for such observers was at once felt on the AISNE, and later the employment of F.O.Os. became general.

Lack of cable and telephones really precluded the extensive employment of F.O.Os.

The Germans were far better provided with telephonic communications in 1914, and showed the greatest enterprise in the employment of F.O.Os.

6. Artillery in the attack.

Field Artillery Training, 1914, divided the artillery action in support of an attack into three arbitrary phases, namely :—

i. The preliminary infantry advance and the artillery duel.

In 1914, it was considered that during this phase the enemy's guns would be disclosed and would open on our infantry, probably firing from positions in the open. The task of the artillery in 1914 at this stage was to silence the enemy's guns, *e.g.*, to carry out intensive counter-battery work. There is no doubt that, in consequence, in many cases our field batteries on the AISNE searched blindly for the German artillery, which very early in 1914 had realized the necessity for occupying covered positions.

F.S.R., 1909, only contemplated an artillery duel in this phase, if the enemy's guns were in fact active.

"The task of the artillery at this stage will usually be to locate the enemy's batteries and, by subduing the fire of those in action, to support the infantry" (F.A.T., 1914, Sec. 155, 2).

"The primary object being to assist the infantry to close with the enemy, an artillery engagement should not be entered into at this stage for its own sake" (F.A.T., 1914, Sec. 155, 3).

ii. The advance of the infantry to the position for the infantry fire fight.

At this stage, it was the task of the artillery to engage the hostile infantry and so help forward the advance of our own infantry to a position preparatory to the assault.

In this phase, the 1914 regulations advocated judicious distribution rather than concentration of artillery fire.

iii The assault.

In 1914, there was no idea of a heavy bombardment before and during the assault.

Broadly speaking, phases (i) and (ii) are now included in :—

(*a*) The contact phases of the battle, where the advanced troops fight their way forward supported by boldly handled artillery using, for the most part, observed fire, fire plans being as simple as compatible with the situation ;

(*b*) The subsequent phase, where, after the enemy's main position has been located and fixed and a comprehensive plan for its capture becomes necessary, the assaulting troops are given a starting line. Their advance from this line is covered by a co-ordinated fire plan which includes both counter-battery and neutralizing fire.

III

SUMMARY OF THE BATTLE, 12TH/15TH SEPTEMBER

12TH SEPTEMBER

1. Orders for 12th September.

In accordance with instructions received from Joffre, the B.E.F. in conjunction with the French Sixth Army on the left and the French Fifth Army on the right, was to continue the advance on 12th, the boundaries for the B.E.F. being BAZOCHES 9279—CRAONNE 0695 on the right and SOISSONS—LAON on the left. G.H.Q. orders were issued at 1800 hours on 11th, Corps being ordered to seize the AISNE crossings, the main columns reaching the high ground overlooking the river.

2. Operations on 12th September.

During the day opposition was met by the leading cavalry on the line of the VESLE between BAZOCHES and CIRY 8286, but with the assistance of the leading troops of the 1, 2 and 3 Divs. at BAZOCHES, COURCELLES 8883 and BRAINE 8783 respectively, the high ground south of the AISNE was reached.

On the left III Corps occupied the plateau south of VENIZEL 7786, the leading troops of 4 Div. reaching the bridge at that place, which was defended by hostile infantry entrenched on the northern bank.

Thus by the end of the day, although the high ground overlooking the river had been reached, none of the crossings were in British hands, except that at VENIZEL, which was captured during the night by 11 Inf. Bde. of 4 Div.

It had rained heavily all day and the roads were heavy with mud.

3. Situation, B.E.F., at nightfall (*see* Map No. 1).

 Cav. Div. and I Corps :—DHUIZEL 9286, LONGUEVAL 9585, COURCELLES.
 3 and 5 Cav. Bdes. :—CHASSEMY 8487, CIRY 8286.
 II Corps :—BRENELLE 8886, BRAINE, CHACRISE 7879, SERCHES 8183.
 III Corps :—BILLY 7684, SEPTMONTS 7482, BUZANCY 7380.

The distances covered by formations as a whole on the 12th were as follow :—

  1 Cav. Bde. .. .. $11\frac{1}{2}$ miles.
  2 Cav. Bde. .. .. $13\frac{1}{2}$ miles.
  4 Cav. Bde. .. .. 10 miles.
  3 Cav. Bde. .. .. 12 miles.
  5 Cav. Bde. .. .. $7\frac{1}{2}$ miles.

1 Div...	19 miles.
2 Div...	17 miles.
3 Div...	15 miles.
5 Div...	8 miles.
4 Div...	15 miles.
19 Inf. Bde...	14½ miles.

4. French situation at night.

On the right, the French Fifth Army was on the VESLE from BEAUMONT to FISMES 9779.

On the left, the French Sixth Army had reached the AISNE from SOISSONS to COMPIEGNE.

5. German situation at night.

On the east, the right of the German Second Army (13 Div.) had been driven back by the French Fifth Army, in touch with British I Corps, and its flank was in danger of being turned.

Von Bülow, therefore, evacuated REIMS during the night, and withdrew his right north of the AISNE to the neighbourhood of BERRY-AU-BAC 1390.

On the west, during 12th, Von Kluck started to sort out his divisions into their proper corps, and occupied a line north of the AISNE as follows :—

VAILLY 8590	Von der Marwitz's Cavalry Corps,
VREGNY 7890	III Corps,
VAUREZIS 6790	II Corps,

with his remaining three corps continuing the line opposite the French Sixth Army almost as far as COMPIEGNE.

Thus by 13th, the gap between the Second and First German Armies had increased to 18 miles, BERRY-AU-BAC to VAILLY, covered only by Von der Marwitz's three cavalry divisions, the Guard, 2nd and 9th.

The German problem was serious. If the gap could not be filled, further retirement would be necessary, and further demoralization entailed. Provided that the gap could be filled, the AISNE afforded a good line on which to stand ; otherwise it would be fatal, as the Allies could penetrate between the two armies.

Von Moltke decided to stand on the AISNE and the following arrangements were made :—

VII Reserve Corps (Von Zwehl), freed by the surrender of MAUBEUGE, to come up on Von Kluck's left (arrived about BRAYE 9293 on 13th).

XV Corps, temporarily detained at BRUSSELS, to fill the remainder of the gap (leading division reached CORBENY 0796 about 1300 hrs. on 14th).

13TH SEPTEMBER

6. Orders for 13th September.

Joffre's Special Instruction No. 23, received at G.H.Q. at 1400 hrs., 12 Sep., directed that the advance be continued in conjunction with the French Fifth and Sixth Armies. The B.E.F. was allotted " the zone included between the road SOISSONS—COUCY LE CHATEAU 9003—SAINT COBLAIN—LA FERE (inclusive) and the road LONGUEVAL—BOURG ET COMIN 9589—CHAMOUILLE 9697—BRUYERES 9604—ATHIES 9709 (inclusive)."

G.H.Q. orders were issued at 1945 hrs., 12 Sep., at COULOMMIERS and directed that " the Army will continue the pursuit to-morrow at seven a.m. Heads of Corps will reach the line LIERVAL 9299—CHAVIGNON 8698—TERNY 7394."

Crossings over the AISNE were allotted as follows :—Cav. Div. and I Corps: BOURG 9589, PONT ARCY 9389, CHAVONNE 8890. 3 and 5 Cav. Bdes. and II Corps: VAILLY 8590, CONDE 8289, MISSY 7987. III Corps: VENIZEL 7686, SOISSONS (later transferred to the French Sixth Army).

7. Operations on 13th September.

The morning was wet and miserable though the weather cleared later in the day. The German resistance was found to be much stronger than anticipated. (VII Res. Corps arrived opposite British I Corps during the afternoon, *see* Stand No. 6, para. 8). I Corps alone made good progress and by the evening were firmly established North of the AISNE. II Corps was strongly opposed and subjected to severe artillery fire when attempting to cross the river. All divisions, however, managed to secure a footing on the north bank.

The positions reached were as follows (*see* map No. 1) :—

I Corps :—
    1 Div.   PAISSY 9993—MOULINS 9792—BOURG 9589.
    2 Div.   (5 Inf. Bde.). VERNEUIL 9491—SOUPIR 9190.
             (One Coy. 4 Gds. Bde.). CHAVONNE 8890.
             Gap of 3 miles.

II Corps :—
    3 Div. (8 and 9 Inf. Bdes.). ROUGE MAISON 8792—VAUXCELLES 8491.
             Gap of 3 miles.
    5 Div. (two Bns. 13 Inf. Bde.). MISSY 7987.
          (14 and 15 Inf. Bdes.). STE. MARGUERITE 7888.

III Corps :—
    4 Div.   STE. MARGUERITE—CROUY 7489.

The remainder of the troops were South of the Aisne.

14TH SEPTEMBER

8. Orders for 14th September.

Joffre's Special Instruction No. 24 directed the pursuit to be continued energetically in a general northerly direction. G.H.Q. orders were issued at 1800 hrs., 13 Sep., at FERE EN TARDENOIS. The only information they contained regarding the enemy was that the advance on 13th had been against strong rear guards of German III Corps and one or two Cav. Divs. The order went on " the Army will continue the pursuit to-morrow at 6 a.m. Heads of Corps will reach the line LAON—SUZY 8206—FRESNE 7406." Roads were allotted to Corps and the Cav. Div. was directed to " advance in the general direction of COURTECON 9495—LAON " and 3 and 5 Cav. Bdes. towards ALLEMANT 8196.

9. Operations on 14th September.

The day opened with a very heavy mist, which did not clear until about midday. Acting on G.H.Q. orders divisions commenced the advance in column of route covered by advanced guards, expecting to be opposed only by enemy rear guards. They found, however, the enemy holding strong positions, entrenched and supported by heavy artillery. In consequence, formations came into action piecemeal to support their advanced guards with little support from their artillery, owing partly to the mist but mainly because of the conformation of the ground. It was a day of hard fighting with little co-ordination between the attacks. On the front of I Corps and 3 Div. the enemy launched many counter-attacks and it was only with difficulty that positions were maintained a little in advance of those of the previous night.

The chief progress had been made on I Corps front, but even there at very great cost. A gap of $1\frac{1}{2}$ miles existed between I and II Corps, only filled by battle outposts of 1 Cav. Bde. II Corps itself was divided into two separate fronts by the CHIVRES 8089 spur, and 5 and 4 Divs. to the westward held a precarious position north of the river with little room for manoeuvre. Every battalion of the B.E.F. was in the line with the exception of those of 19 Inf. Bde., not a single permanent bridge over the river was available, and the temporary bridges were liable to destruction by flood. Fortunately, the enemy was in an equally difficult position; VII Res. Corps had only one battalion in reserve.

The approximate position of the forward troops at night was (see Map No. 2) :—

I Corps :—
    1 Div. .. CHEMIN DES DAMES N.E. of TROYON 9694—BEAULNE 9392.
    2 Div. .. BEAULNE (Excl.)—LA BOVETTE 9192—pt. 166 north of CHAVONNE 8890.
    1 and 2 Cav. Bdes.—Linking up left of 2 Div. with right of 3 Div.

II Corps :—
- 3 Div. .. Mill 1 mile west of CHAVONNE 8890—ROUGE MAISON 8792—VAUXCELLES Chateau 8491—south to the AISNE.
- 5 Div. .. MISSY 7987—STE. MARGUERITE 7888.

III Corps :—
- 4 Div. .. STE. MARGUERITE 7888—LA MONTAIGNE FM. 7789—pt. 151 west of CROUY 7489.

15TH SEPTEMBER

10. G.H.Q. orders were for all troops to entrench on the positions occupied and for the concentration of the heavy batteries on those of the enemy.

It was a day of German counter-attacks, all of which were repulsed. A final attempt was made by 5 Div. to capture CHIVRES spur but without success.

The positions gained on 14th were substantially the same as those handed over to the French when the B.E.F. was withdrawn from the AISNE a few weeks later.

Details of the battle are given in Part IV.

IV

TOUR OF THE BATTLEFIELD WITH INCIDENTS IN THE BATTLE

The incidents in the battle given below are arranged under the heading of selected view points, whence a general view over the ground where they took place can be obtained. These stands are marked on Map No. 1.

There are, however, many other points from which particular incidents in the battle can be followed.

Stand No. 1.

Spur ½ mile south of BILLY, about 759838. It is best approached by a footpath from the road to the west starting about 762837.

Operations of 4th Div., 12 Sep.

1. From this point a view is obtained of the high ground north of the river from CHIVRES spur, 7989, on the right to CROUY 7489 on the left, and also of the AISNE valley with VENIZEL, 7686, and BILLY 7684. The difficulties of an attack across the flat ground by day can well be appreciated.

2. 4 Div.—12 Sep.

For the night 11/12 Sep., 4 Div. were at LA LOGE FARM, 6670, and CHOUY, 6668. The march on 12 Sep. in heavy rain and over heavy roads was very trying. The leading Inf. Bde. (12) reached the high ground north of SEPTMONTS, 7482, overlooking the AISNE at 1500 hrs. The Div. Cav. reported that the bridge at VENIZEL, though damaged, was passable; that enemy trenches were just to the north of it and a column of Germans was moving N.E. from SOISSONS. 31 Hy. Bty. came into action at 1630 hrs. 1 mile N.E. of SEPTMONTS and endeavoured to catch this column. A battery of 29 Bde. R.F.A. went into action about 1600 hrs. $\frac{1}{2}$ mile south of BILLY to support an advance on VENIZEL, but the light failed early and outposts (12 Inf. Bde.) were put out on the edge of the high ground overlooking the AISNE. A party of 2 Inniskg. was sent down to the bridge by the initiative of the battalion commander, Major C. A. Wilding. On their arrival the Germans attempted to destroy it but the charges did not all explode and Captain S. A. Roe removed the fuzes by the light of an electric torch, within close range of the Germans entrenched on the northern bank. The remainder of the Div. went into billets about SEPTMONTS.

3. 4 Div.—Night 12/13 Sep.

About 2100 hrs. Brig. Gen. Hunter-Weston, commanding 11 Inf. Bde., after a conference at Div. H.Q., SEPTMONTS, was instructed to push forward and seize a crossing at VENIZEL bridge. He at once sent two officers down to the bridge; one was to find out the condition of the bridge and remain there while the other was to return with a guide to lead the brigade. The brigade marched off at 2300 hrs. led by the brigade commander. At CARRIERE L'EVEQUE FM., 7483, the junior infantry reconnaissance officer met the column but was completely exhausted and had dismissed the guide. Brig. Gen. Hunter-Weston led the brigade himself by map, arriving at VENIZEL at 0100 hrs., 13 Sep. It was still raining hard.

The R.E. officer reported that, although the main girders of the bridge had been cut, the concrete roadway was probably strong enough to carry infantry if great care were taken. German trenches on the south bank of the river were unoccupied and, though a patrol had been seen, it had retired after firing a few shots.

There were now four hours left before daylight. After inspecting the bridge himself and studying the map, the brigade commander decided that to occupy a bridge head on the flat ground just north of the bridge would be of little value, for an attack on the high ground by day would be sure to entail heavy casualties. He considered it necessary to get a footing on the crest before daylight.

1 Hamps. were sent over first to take up a covering position. 1 R.B., 1 Som. L.I. and 1 E. Lan. R. followed in single file and were assembled in close column in the open a few hundred yards north of the river. Ammunition limbers were unloaded and their contents taken over by hand. The movement was complete by 0300 hrs.

Brig. Gen. Hunter-Weston issued orders for 1 R.B. to seize the spur north of STE. MARGUERITE 7888, 1 Hamps. the MONTAGNE FME., 7789, spur and 1 Som. L.I. the spur west of CROUY, 1 E. Lan. R. to be in reserve at BUCY LE LONG 7688.

The battalions fixed bayonets and moved off independently covered by small advanced guards. As they advanced, there was just enough light to see the outline of the spurs on which they were directed. They reached the crest as dawn was breaking, and the Germans made no attempt to hold their advanced trenches but retired to their main position several hundred yards to the north.

" It was a most satisfactory end to a trying march of some thirty miles through pouring rain in a temperature more appropriate to November than early Autumn, with little or no food for more than twenty-four hours. Had other divisions been equally enterprising —and their marches on 12th had been shorter than those of the 4th Division—the fighting on 13th might have had a different result."—Official History.

Stand No. 2.

VENIZEL bridge.

1. The points worthy of attention here are :—
    (a) The width of the river.
    (b) The flat ground north of the river.
    (c) The way in which the high ground north of the river commands the bridge and the ground immediately to the north of it.
    (d) The difficulty there would have been in advancing had the crossing been contested by the Germans.

2. H.Q. 4 Div. on 14 Sep. was in a café near the south end of the bridge. A place more liable to be shelled could hardly have been chosen, but it remained untouched for some time.

Stand No. 3.

LA MONTAGNE FM. 772892 facing south.

Operations of 4 Div. 13/15 Sep.

1. The field of view from this point shows again how costly an attack across the open plain north of VENIZEL would have been had the Germans held this ground. It is difficult to understand why they did not do so. The view has been advanced that, as their peace training required a single strong line with a long field of fire, they put their main position well back from the ridge. They could, however, have obtained this equally well by holding the edge of the plateau. Perhaps the answer is that on the night of 12th the subordinate commanders were expecting to continue the retirement on 13th.

The importance of CHIVRES spur, which dominates the AISNE valley, is obvious from this point.

4 Div.—13 Sep.

2. 12 Inf. Bde. began at 0600 hrs. to cross at VENIZEL bridge, which had by now been made somewhat safer. At the same time a French brigade was crossing at SOISSONS. 12 Inf. Bde. was harassed by German 8-inch and 5-9-inch batteries, chiefly from CHIVRES spur. By 1100 hrs. the brigade (except 1 Inniskg. Fus. left to bring the guns over the bridge) was across and had begun to advance in widely extended order on BUCY LE LONG, under heavy shrapnel fire which, however, did little damage. A vivid description of this advance as it appeared to the Germans on CHIVRES spur is given by Bloem (*see* Official History, page 383). 68 Bty. R.F.A. followed 12 Inf. Bde. to BUCY LE LONG.

3. 10 Inf. Bde. took up a covering position along the railway embankment between VENIZEL and VILLENEUVE 7487.

4. 11 Inf. Bde. remained in its position unmolested all day. Some of 1 R.B. had by mid-day worked through the woods on the eastern side of the STE. MARGUERITE spur and were enfilading the German trenches on the slopes of the CHIVRES spur.

5. At about 1430 hrs. 12 Inf. Bde. advanced to attack CHIVRES spur from STE. MARGUERITE with the Essex on the right of the road and L. F. on the left. By 1200 hrs. R.E. of 5 Div. had built a raft to carry 60 men at MOULIN DES ROCHES 7886, and 2 Manch. followed by Surreys (14 Inf. Bde.) crossed the river. At 1500 hrs. both battalions started to advance on the eastern end of STE. MARGUERITE to support 12 Inf. Bde., which had been holding the village. As they were nearing STE. MARGUERITE a request was received from 12 Inf. Bde. to co-operate by attacking CHIVRES spur from the south. They were under heavy shrapnel fire and it was too late to comply. An endeavour was made, however, to change the direction of advance so as to bring the Surreys in on the right of 12 Inf. Bde. with the Manch. in echelon to the right rear. Owing to the difficulty in changing direction these two battalions were not in fact able to render much assistance.

12 Inf. Bde. had by this time begun their advance but progress was slow owing to the swampy ground and thick undergrowth. About 1700 hrs. the L. F. were stopped by fire from trenches south of CHIVRES village and from CHIVRES spur. At this time two guns of 68 Bty. R.F.A. opened fire from the head of the MONCEL ravine, 7789, drawing heavy retaliation on that area. The guns had to retire and some parties of 1 R.B. on STE. MARGUERITE spur were also driven back with considerable loss.

The L. F. held their positions until nightfall, when they were relieved by 2 Manch., having lost 6 officers and 170 men.

6. 10 Inf. Bde. was moved across the river at VENIZEL during the night 13/14 and took up a position on the left of 11 Inf. Bde.

At night 4 Div. held a line from (incl.) STE. MARGUERITE spur facing CHIVRES village to (excl.) CROUY.

7. Artillery of 4 Div.—13 Sep.

(a) 29 Bde. R.F.A.

126 Bty. in action near BILLY, fired 220 rounds, mostly at hostile batteries at extreme range.

125 and 127 Btys. in action near LE CARRIER, 7784.

(b) 14 Bde. R.F.A. and 35 How. Bty. at 0430 in readiness S.W. of ACY, 7783.

68 Bty. accompanied 12 Inf. Bde., and, after the section that opened fire from MONCEL ravine was forced to retire, dug in just north of VENIZEL.

88 Bty. had four guns in action at LA MONTAGNE FME. at dusk but did not fire.

39 Bty. and 1 Sec. 88 Bty. joined 68 Bty. N.E. of VENIZEL at dusk.

35 How. Bty. at 2000 hrs. in action behind the wood west of MOULIN DES ROCHES.

(c) 37 How. Bde. (less 35 Bty.).

In action near LE CARRIER but fired little or nothing all day.

(d) 32 Bde. R.F.A. was attached to Cav. Div.

(e) 31 Hy. Bty. in action 1 mile N.W. of CARRIERE L'EYEQUE FME., and engaged hostile btys. of German 3 Div. with success.

Thus the infantry of 4 Div. had practically no artillery support during the day. Owing to the width of the valley this was almost inevitable, but perhaps more use might have been made of the 4·5-inch How., which could have found suitable positions further forward.

8. 4 Div.—14 Sep.

4 Div. received orders to push northward over the plateau between VREGNY 7891 and CROUY to help forward both 5 Div. on the right and French 45 Div. on the left. The divisional commander decided that, owing to the impossibility of giving artillery support, he was not justified in making an attack against the German position, which was strongly entrenched, until the divisions on his flanks made some progress. As the attacks of both these divisions were unsuccessful, 4 Div. made no attempt to advance.

During the day 4 Div. was subjected to intermittent artillery fire. There were few casualties except in 10 Inf. Bde., which lost 100 officers and men. At noon the intensity of the enemy fire on LA MONTAGNE FME. caused apprehension of an attack and a company of the Dublins was sent forward. After advancing ½ mile they engaged hostile infantry at 400 yards range and silenced its fire.

9. **Artillery of 4 Div.—14. Sep.**

(a) 37 How. Bde. R.F.A.

31 and 55 How. Btys. crossed before dawn and came into action in the valley west of LA MONTAGNE FME. with an OP. giving good observation towards CROUY though not to the north. They kept three enemy batteries on the heights beyond CROUY quiet all the morning. About noon, after a German aeroplane had fired a Very light over 31 Bty., 21-cm. shells began to fall on the battery. This continued all the afternoon and, although no guns were put out of action. 17 men and 35 horses were killed.

(b) 29 Bde. R.F.A.

126 Bty. crossed the river but, as no suitable position could be found, it did not fire and returned south of the river.

125 and 127 Btys. moved to positions on the spur S.W. of SERMOISE, 8086, to assist 5 Div. attack.

(c) 14 Bde. R.F.A.

68 Bty. was severely shelled during the day and was withdrawn south of the river at night.

88 Bty. was in position north of BUCY LE LONG but did not fire all day.

39 Bty. was in reserve at BUCY LE LONG.

(d) 31 Hy. Bty. left its position just south of ACY at 1100 hrs. to join 5 Div.

10. **4 Div.—15 Sep.**

There was no change in the situation. The day was spent entrenching and wiring.

Note.—It is best to move to Stand No. 4, STE. MARGUERITE, via PONT ROUGE, 7792, VREGNY, 7990, and CHIVRES, 7989. During the journey the approximate position of the German line and battery positions can be seen and the difficult nature of the ground in the CHIVRES valley appreciated.

Stand No. 4.

STE. MARGUERITE. On the slope of the spur about 797888.

Operations of 5 Div.

1. From this point a view of the ground over which the attack of 12 Inf. Bde. was made is obtained. Other points to note are VENIZEL, MOULINS DES ROCHES, ACY spur, SERMOISE and the spur S.W. of it, R. VESLE, BRAINE and the direction of SERCHES 8083.

2. 5 Div.—12 Sep.

On the night 11/12, 5 Div. were at HARTENNES, 7475, and BILLY SUR OURCQ, 7069. The march on 12th was covered by 3 and 5 Cav. Bdes. (Gough's Cavalry). Owing to the weather conditions the head of 5 Div. only arrived at SERCHES, with the remainder of the division extending to NAMPTEUIL, 8078, before it halted for the night. No attempt was made to get across the river that night. The cavalry had found CONDE 8289 bridge intact but strongly held.

3. 5 Div.—13 Sep.

5 Div. was allotted the bridges at CONDE and MISSY 8087, 4 miles apart. Although CONDE bridge was intact, the approaches were very exposed. It was decided to advance only on MISSY.

4. Cyclist Coy. 4 Div. had seized MISSY bridge at 0100 hrs. and left a party to hold it. At 0400 hrs. this party were driven off and the Germans reoccupied their positions and destroyed the bridge.

5. About 0600 hrs. two Coys. R.W.K. (13 Inf. Bde.) approached the bridge but found it defended by hidden machine guns, which they engaged and compelled to retire. The bridge was examined by a party of 59 Fd. Coy. R.E., who found that three spans had been destroyed. The party were then driven off by fire and the two Coys. R.W.K. entrenched to the east of the bridge. H.Q. 13 Inf. Bde. were behind a haystack 500 yards south of the **G.** in LA GOBINNE, 8087.

6. Owing to a misunderstanding, a demonstration which was to have been made against CONDE bridge by Gough's Cavalry did not take place.

7. The R.W.K. were unable to move from their trenches until nightfall, when they began to dribble men across by boat, and later by rafts constructed by 59 Fd. Coy. When about 40 men were over, a German patrol was met and anihilated; this saved the movement from interruption. By daylight 14 Sep. the R.W.K. and K.O.S.B. were across and entrenched in a wood on the north bank. The two other battalions of the brigade remained at CIRY 6286 and SERMOISE.

8. While 13 Inf. Bde. were held up at MISSY, 14 Inf. Bde. moved down towards MOULINS DES ROCHES where two battalions crossed by raft as described at Stand 3, para. 5. The rest of the brigade crossed during the afternoon and was followed by 15 Inf. Bde. starting at 2100 hrs. Both 14 and 15 Inf. Bdes. were concentrated about STE. MARGUERITE by 0600 hrs., 14 Sep.

9. Artillery 5 Div.—13 Sep.

(26 Field guns had been lost at LE CATEAU.)

(a) 27 Bde. R.F.A. was with 13 Inf. Bde.

119 and 120 Btys. came into action above SERCHES 8083, and engaged enemy artillery on CHIVRES plateau with success.

121 Bty. had one section in action just west of SERMOISE but it was shelled out. Later the battery came into action about 816863.

(b) 15 Bde. R.F.A.

Consisting only of 11 and 80 Btys. of 4 guns each, the brigade together with 61 How. Bty. was grouped with 14 Inf. Bde.

The brigade was in action from about noon near JURY, 7984.

(c) 65 and 37 How. Btys., under the C.R.A., were in action on the SERCHES plateau.

108 Hy. Bde. at noon was in action east of SERCHES, searching for 5·9-inch Hows. which were shelling 13 Inf. Bde. During the afternoon the battery was shelled and took up a position further back.

(d) No artillery crossed the river on 13th. It will be seen that 5 Div. Arty. had not the same difficulties as had that of 2, 3 and 4 Divs. They were within range of CHIVRES spur and observation was fairly good.

10. 5 Div.—14 Sep.

5 Div. operation orders were for the continuation of the pursuit to destinations 15 miles to the north. It early became evident that these orders could not be carried out so long as CHIVRES spur remained in the hands of the enemy. A plan was therefore made to attack as follows :—

14 Inf. Bde. eastward from STE. MARGUERITE with its right thrown forward to threaten CHIVRES spur from the south.

R.W.K. and K.O.S.B. (13 Inf. Bde.) to co-operate on the right.

15 Inf. Bde., when right of 14 Inf. Bde. had cleared MISSY, to pass through that village and attack from S.E.

15 Bde. R.F.A. and 8 How. Bde. R.F.A. (each less one bty.) to support the attack from the vicinity of BUCY LE LONG.

11. The 14 Inf. Bde. attack made slow progress owing to heavy artillery and machine gun fire. 2 Manch. on the left were held up by enfilade fire from CHIVRES, but at 1200 hrs. D.C.L.I. in the centre and Surreys on the right had established themselves on the north edge of MISSY. One company was sent out to feel for 13 Inf. Bde. on the right. The two battalions of this brigade,

however, were checked by fire on the north bank near MISSY bridge and took no part in the attack.

15 Inf. Bde. left the Dorsets in the sunken road north of STE. MARGUERITE and the head of the brigade arrived at MISSY about 1430 hrs. One Coy. Bedfs. with one Coy. Surreys were then sent well up the spur above MISSY. There was considerable delay owing to shell fire and dispositions for the attack were not ready until 1630 hrs.

Owing to the left centre of 14 Inf. Bde. having been stopped by both frontal and flanking fire, it was decided to make the new attack from the south only. Ten Coys. of both brigades took part. The Bedfs. and Surreys on the left made good progress. But on the right, owing to insufficient time to get to the starting points, the wire obstacles in the woods and the woods being shelled by both sides, the attack became confused and the order was given to abandon it. An account of this action is given by Bloem, pages 184-194.

By nightfall 14 Inf. Bde. had taken up a line from STE. MARGUERITE to MISSY which was continued to MISSY bridge by R.W.K. (13 Inf. Bde.). 15 Inf. Bde. was reformed and bivouacked in MISSY.

12. **Artillery 5 Div.—14 Sep.**

(a) 8 How. Bde. R.F.A.
    61 Bty. took up a position near the sunken lane running north from the east end of STE. MARGUERITE with an O.P. near this stand.
    37 Bty. had no orders. One section came into action between STE. MARGUERITE and the railway but was immediately neutralised.
    65 Bty. (under the C.R.A.) was on VASSENY spur 8284.

(b) 15 Bde. R.F.A. had its two btys. in action at BUCY LE LONG in close support of 14 Inf. Bde.

(c) 27 Bde. R.F.A. and 108 Hy. Bty. were in action south of the river.

13. **5 Div.—15 Sep.**

Orders were issued for 14 and 15 Inf. Bdes. to renew their attack over the same ground as before, while 13 Inf. Bde. attacked from the south-east.

The D.W.R. crossed the river at MISSY by raft but 13 Inf. Bde. found it impossible to move down the CONDE road owing to artillery and machine gun fire and consequently could not reach its position to take part in the attack. 2 K.O.Y.L.I. did not cross the river as its rafts were not ready.

15 Inf. Bde. attacked with 1 Norfolk, 1 Bedfs. being in support. It was soon found that the enemy had put up additional defences

in the woods and in spite of artillery bombardment lasting half an hour the attack came to a standstill.

The advance of 14 Inf. Bde. with 1 D.C.L.I. and 2 Manch. was also stopped by fire from the spur.

At 1000 hrs. congestion of the reserve battalions of 14 and 15 Inf. Bdes. in MISSY was spotted by an enemy aeroplane and the village was so heavily shelled that it had to be evacuated.

At 1100 hrs. Brig. Gen. Rolt (14 Inf. Bde.) was put in command of all troops north of the river. It was later decided to consolidate the line MISSY—STE. MARGUERITE and during the night 15 Inf. Bde. was withdrawn to reserve south of the river.

Stand No. 5.

Spur just north of CONDE village, about 824898.

Operations of 3 Div.

1. From here a view to the east up the AISNE valley is obtained, and most of the ground over which 3 Div. operated can be seen.

2. 3 Div.—12 Sep.

On 12 Sep., 3 Div. marched from GRAND ROZOY, 7671, and OULCHY LA VILLE, 7368, to BRENELLE, 8786, and BRAINE, 8783, where it went into billets for the night 12/13 Sep.

3. 3 Div.—13 Sep.

For the advance on 13 Sept., 3 Div. was allotted the crossings over the AISNE river and canal at VAILLY, 8590. The canal bridge was intact but the river bridge and a light railway bridge a mile up stream were destroyed.

8 Inf. Bde. advanced at 0700 hrs. but was checked at the edge of the plateau above CHASSEMY, 8487, by artillery fire from CHIVRES spur. At 1000 hrs. the R.S. worked down through the woods to the canal near the bridge. It was then found that the gap in the river bridge was spanned by a plank footway.

At 1300 hrs. the divisional commander, after a personal reconnaissance of the bridges, ordered 8 Inf. Bde. to advance, but it was not until 1500 hrs. that the R.S. and R. Irish began to cross the river. They were steadily shelled while doing so but by 1600 hrs. the R.S. were established at VAUXELLES chateau, 8491, with outposts on the southern slopes of JOUY spur, 8594. Before nightfall the rest of 8 Inf. Bde. was at ST. PIERRE 8491.

After dark 9 Inf. Bde. crossed and took up a line of outposts from ROUGE MAISON, 8792, westwards. These brigades moved in single file over the plank bridge and had to leave their transport south of the river. During the night the R.E. began the construction of a pontoon bridge.

7 Inf. Bde. remained at BRAINE about 6 miles by road from the river.

4. Artillery 3 Div.—13 Sep.
- (a) 40 Bde. R.F.A. was with 8 Inf. Bde. but only 49 Bty. came into action south of CHASSEMY. It was heavily shelled and two guns were put out of action.
- (b) 30 (How.) Bde.
   129 Bty. at LA GRANGE FM., 8584.
   130 Bty. 2,000 yards east of CHASSEMY.
   128 Bty. in CHASSEMY CHATEAU grounds.
- (c) 23 Bde. R.F.A. had two batteries in action N.E. of CHASSEMY.
- (d) 42 Bde. R.F.A. with 7 Inf. Bde. did not fire all day.
- (e) 48 Hy. Bty. in action just north of BRENELLE.

The position the 3 Div. Arty. was very unfavourable. To obtain cover, batteries could not be placed further forward than the southern edge of the BRENELLE plateau, more than two miles behind the infantry; even so, the VESLE valley was under observation from CHIVRES spur. As there were no positions north of the river, only the 60-prs. could do counter-battery work. The lack of cable rendered the use of F.O.Os. almost impossible and, though flag signalling was attempted, it was not very successful.

5. 3 Div.—14 Sep.

Orders were for 3 Div. to continue the pursuit.

At dawn the R. S. (8 Inf. Bde.) advanced to take up a position on the crest of JOUY spur. On reaching it they came under fire at close range. The R. Irish were brought up on their right, 4 Mx. on their left. They were practically without artillery support and came to a standstill just short of the crest. (The combined strength of these three battalions was only 1500.) 40 Fd. Bde. had crossed the river but could find no position.

About 0900 hrs. the enemy attacked 8 Inf. Bde. and at 1000 hrs. the brigade began to fall back to the south of JOUY spur.
7 Inf. Bde. was ordered forward in support but, on approaching VAILLY bridge, as the shell fire was so heavy, the brigade was diverted by its commander to cross by the light railway bridge which now had a plank footway across the gap. The delay this caused deprived 8 Inf. Bde. of its support.

6. Meanwhile about 0700 hrs. the enemy, covered by artillery and machine gun fire, attacked the Lincolns and R. F. (9 Inf. Bde.) at ROUGE MAISON. The N. F. were sent up on the left and the three battalions were ordered to advance in counter-attack. On emerging from the woods, all were met by heavy fire and, after attempting to entrench, were forced back and clung to the edge of the spur. The R. S. F., the last reserve, were thrown in, two companies on either flank.

7. The situation was now critical. The right of 9 Inf. Bde. was exposed and there was a gap of $1\frac{1}{2}$ miles to the left of 2 Div. on

CHAVONNE spur. Our artillery, south of the river, was useless owing to mist and the only troops to fill the gaps were the Greys and 12 L. (5 Cav. Bde.), which were in VAILLY, having crossed in the early morning. The Germans, however, were unable to press their attack on this flank and so missed the opportunity of splitting I Corps from the remainder of the B.E.F.

8. By 1300 hrs. 1 Wilts. (7 Inf. Bde.) had crossed the river and pushed forward on to the ST. PRECORD spur, 8691, on the right of 9 Inf. Bde. It was followed by 2 R.Ir. Rifles at 1530 hrs. The position was now stabilized and the remainder of 7 Inf. Bde. moved into reserve at VAILLY, and owing to the satisfactory situation 5 Cav. Bde. were ordered south of the river.

The enemy artillery had been very active all day. It did some effective counter-battery work as well as close support of the infantry and shelled VAILLY pontoon bridge all the morning, finally destroying it at about 1300 hrs.

9. Artillery 3 Div.—14 Sep.

(a) 40 Bde., after being unable to find positions north of the river, re-crossed at PONT ARCY, 9289, about 1400 hrs. and eventually came into position on the BRENELLE plateau at dusk. It fired nothing all day.

(b) 42 Bde. had 29 and 41 btys. in action east of CHASSEMY; 45 bty. was in readiness as shown on tracing, but did not come into action.

(c) 23 Bde., 107 and 108 Btys., in action on BRENELLE plateau, 109 came into action near pt. 165, 8787, against a counter-attack, but was soon neutralized.

(d) 30 How. Bde., in action about CHASSEMY chateau. 128 and 129 Btys. endeavoured unsuccessfully to silence enemy batteries shelling the bridge. 130 Bty. from a position 1000 yards east of CHASSEMY fired 2000 rounds at enemy infantry and the edges of the woods above CELLES 8290 and about ROUGE MAISON.

(e) 48 Hy. Bty. in action just north of BRENELLE. The Staff Captain, 9 Inf. Bde., was sent back and pointed out areas in which hostile machine guns were active. These areas and machine guns at FOLEMPRISE FM., 8892, were shelled, and also enemy counter-attacking. The battery was heavily shelled and moved 500 yards further back at night.

(f) C.R.A. had his H.Q. on BRENELLE plateau keeping touch with his brigades by orderly.

10. 3 Div.—15 Sep.

In the early morning 7 Inf. Bde. discovered the enemy entrenching between LA FOSSE MARQUET, 8791, and ROUGE MAISON. Two companies of R. Ir. Rifles tried to clear them out of the wood between the two places but were repulsed with heavy loss.

During the day the enemy made several attacks and demonstrations, but these were all repulsed by rifle and machine gun fire. The bridge at VAILLY was repaired and made passable by wheels.

Stand No. 6.

The crest of the spur west of VIEIL ARCY, about 924875.

Operations of 1 and 2 Divs., 12 and 13 Sep., and of 2 Div., 14 Sep.

From this point a view of the whole front of I Corps from BOURG 8589 to CHAVONNE 8890 is obtained.

1. **I Corps and Cav. Div.—12 Sep.**

The areas occupied for the night 11/12 were:—

Cav. Div. ..	LOUPEIGNE, 8772, westward to ARCY STE. RESTITUE, 8273.
1 Div. ..	BRUYERES, 8066—VILLENEUVE, 8265.
2 Div. ..	BEUGNEUX, 7871—OULCHY, 7567. LE CHATEAU, 7467.

During the advance on the 12th, 1 Cav. Bde. had an engagement with enemy rear guards at BRAINE which occupied about two hours, but, though the advanced guard of 2 Div. had reached MONTHUSSART FM., 8984, by 1330 hrs., neither cavalry or infantry reached the AISNE that night.

The billets occupied for the night were:—

1 Cav. Div.	DHUIZEL, 9286, VILLERS EN PRAYERES, 9787, VAUXTIN, 9284.
1 Div. ..	LONGUEVAL, 9585. PAARS, 9281.
2 Div. ..	DHUIZEL, 9286, COURCELLES, 8983.

I Corps and Cav. Div.—13 Sep.

2. The orders issued by I Corps were for the advance to be continued. 1 Div. was to cross at BOURG, 2 Div. at PONT ARCY and CHAVONNE. Patrols were to be pushed down to the river by daylight and divisions were to close up with a view to following up the enemy or, if a resistance was put up, of making an attack under corps orders. No specific duties were allotted to the Cav. Div. by G.H.Q. It continued to co-operate with I Corps.

3. **1 Div.**

2 Cav. Bde. led the way against the BOURG crossing. The river bridges were broken but the canal bridges were intact. At BOURG, however, it was possible to cross by the tow path of the canal aqueduct over the river, which would also take guns. Opposition was encountered but with the assistance of 2 Inf. Bde. the crossing was effected. 2 Cav. Bde. at once occupied the BOURG

spur while 1 Cav. Bde., which followed, struck east towards PARGNAN 9790 to gain touch with the French. I Bty. R.H.A. crossed with 2 Cav. Bde. and opened fire on a German column seen moving north from VENDRESSE 9693. German artillery retaliated and drove 2 Cav. Bde. back to the south side of BOURG spur.

2 Inf. Bde. crossed the river after the cavalry and by 1300 hrs. had reached the top of BOURG spur. This enabled 2 Cav. Bde. to push on to MOULINS 9692, where it was checked by enemy holding the TROYON spur 9794. At this time hostile troops were reported by the R.F.C. concentrating north of COURTECON 9495 while others were seen moving from CHIVY 9493 on BOURG. In consequence, 1 (Guards) and 3 Inf. Bdes. were ordered across the river and directed north-east on PAISSY 9993.

By 1800 hrs. the whole of 1 Div. was across the river and at nightfall the situation was :—

    1 (Guards) Bde. on PAISSY spur holding the village.
    2 Inf. Bde. from (incl.) MOULINS down the BOURG spur.

2 Cav. Bde. with 3 Inf. Bde. and 1 Div. Tps. went into billets in OEUILLY 9789 and BOURG while 1 Cav. Bde. re-crossed the river at PONT ARCY.

4. Artillery 1 Div.—13 Sep.

(a) 25 Bde. R.F.A. and 30 How. Bty. with 2 Inf. Bde. crossed the river about 1400 hrs. and went into action north-east of PARGNAN between 1600 and 1700 hrs. One battery fired at the Germans in TROYON at 1700 hrs.

(b) 39 and 26 Bdes. R.F.A. moved forward during the afternoon to billets at BOURG.

(c) 43 How. Bde. R.F.A. (less 30 Bty.) was in readiness in the PARGNAN area in the evening but did not fire.

(d) 26 Hy. Bty. One section in action above VAUXCERE 9384 fired 44 rounds at the Germans on the CHEMIN DE DAMES. Later the battery moved into BOURG.

It will be seen therefore that 1 and 2 Inf. Bdes. had little or no artillery support during the day.

5. 2 Div.

About 0500 hrs. Div. Cav. reported the canal bridges at CYS 9089 intact ; the river bridge at CHAVONNE destroyed and the approaches covered by snipers on the north bank ; at PONT ARCY the canal bridge slightly damaged and the river bridge destroyed.

5 Inf. Bde. (Adv. Guard of 2 Div.) found, however, that it was possible to get men on foot across, and part of the brigade made their way over almost unopposed. This enabled 5 and 11 Fd. Coys. to commence the construction of a pontoon bridge a little further to the east. The bridge was completed about 1630 hrs., when the remainder of the 5 Inf. Bde. crossed under shell fire. It was not until after

dark that it moved forward towards the left of 1 Div. and took up the position (incl.) VERNEUIL 9491—MOUSSY 9391—SOUPIR 9090.

At about 1200 hrs. 2 Coldm. Gds. (4 Guards Bde.) were sent to secure a crossing at CHAVONNE. Driving in the enemy riflemen the battalion crossed the broken span of the bridge, by a trestle construction left by the Germans, and advanced to the top of the ridge beyond at about 1730 hrs. On this being reported to 2 Div., orders were given for the battalion to withdraw south of the river. The reason for this order is unknown but 1 Div. received direct orders from I Corps to this effect. 4 Guards Bde. therefore went into billets south of the river leaving one Coy. 2 Coldm. Gds. holding a close bridge head at CHAVONNE.

6. Artillery 2 Div.

(a) 41 Bde. R.F.A. in observation west of VIEIL ARCY 9287 to support 5 Inf. Bde.

(b) 34 and 44 (How.) Bdes. R.F.A. in action west and south-west of VIEIL ARCY and DHUIZEL, one bty. of each supported 2 Coldm. Gds. crossing at CHAVONNE.

(c) 36 Bde. R.F.A. was not in action.

(d) 35 Hy. Bty. was in action south-west of VIEIL ARCY at 1100 hrs. and shelled thick masses of the enemy on SOUPIR spur.

None of the 2 Div. Arty. crossed the river.

7. French operations on the right.

French 35 Div. (XVIII Corps) crossed the AISNE at PONTAVERT 0890 about 1030 hrs. Later in the day XVIII Corps were getting on well and were reported attacking towards CORBENY 0796, CRAONNE 0595 and CRAONELLE 0493, though Conneau's Cavalry Corps, which earlier in the day had occupied JUVINCOURT 1395, had fallen back to escape being cut off. Further east the French Ninth Army (Foch) and Fourth Army had made considerable progress.

8. German dispositions.

On the evening of 12th and early morning of 13th a gap existed between the left of Von Kluck's First Army and the right of Von Bülow's Second Army of about 18 miles from VAILLY to BERRY AU BAC 1290. This gap was filled by three cavalry divisions, the Guard, 2 and 9, and was being entered by British I Corps and Cav. Div., by French XVIII Corps and Conneau's Cavalry Corps and Valabregue's group of reserve divisions, a total of four regular divisions, three reserve divisions and four cavalry divisions.

On 8 Sep., German VII Reserve Corps was freed by the surrender of MAUBEUGE and about 0500 hrs., 13 Sep., bivouacked 5 miles south and south-west of LAON after a march of 40 miles in 24 hours. There it had only a brief rest before again advancing, 13 Res. Div.

on BRAYE 7592, and 27 Res. bde. of 14 Res. Div. on CERNY 9795, while 28 Bde. moved further east against the French. They arrived about 1400 hrs. and relieved Von der Marvitz's cavalry corps, which assembled on their left. Thus by the evening of 13th the gap was filled and the opportunity afforded to the Allies was definitely lost. In addition, XV Corps was arriving to join Von Hutingens newly formed Seventh Army. Orders were issued that evening by Von Bülow for a general attack on 14th to consolidate the line of his three armies.

9. Situation, evening of 13 Sep.

Owing to the weather conditions little air reconnaissance was possible on 13th and only one German cavalry division and about two infantry divisions between CERNY and AIZY 8693, and another near LAON, were reported. These were the Guard Cav. Div., 13 Res. Div. (VII Res. Corps) and one division of III Corps.

In accordance with G.H.Q. orders, I corps gave the CHEMIN DES DAMES ridge as the first objective for 14th, 1 Div. from CERNY to COURTECON and 2 Div. thence to BRAYE 9293 tunnel entrance.

The Cav. Div. was ordered to push on to LAON.

I Corps—14 Sep.
10. 1 Div.

As it was known the enemy held the TROYON sugar factory, 968946, 2 Inf. Bde. with two batteries 25 Bde. R.F.A. was ordered to seize the crest from CERNY to TILLEUL DE COURTECON. Under its cover 1 Guards Bde. with one battery and a Fd. Coy., clearing MOULINS at 0730 hrs., was to march on CHAMOUILLE 9698 via CERNY. The rest of the division was to follow, leaving two brigades R.F.A. and 26 Hy. Bty. on PAISSY spur.

The remainder of the operations of 1 Div. are described under Stands Nos. 7 and 8.

11. 2 Div.

2 Div. orders were for 6 Inf. Bde. (with 37 Bde. R.F.A.) to form the advanced guard and to cross at PONT ARCY at 0500 hrs. and advance northward through 5 Inf. Bde., which was then to follow. 4 Guards Bde. (with 36 Bde. R.F.A.) was to cross at PONT ARCY at 0700 hrs. and, turning north-west, to advance along the SOUPIR spur followed by the remainder of the division, except 35 Hy. Bty., which was to cross at BOURG.

Owing to the narrowness of the bridge, 6 Inf. Bde. did not complete crossing until 0800 hrs. The R. Berks advanced up the valley on BRAYE with the protection on each flank of two Coys. 1 K.R.R.C.

About 0900 hrs., on reaching MAISON BRULEE, the R. Berks were held up by artillery and small-arm fire from the main ridge north of BRAYE and the woods on the sides of the valley. 1 Kings were ordered up on the right of the R. Berks, between them and the right detachment K.R.R.C. At 1000 hrs. 34 Bde. R.F.A. came into action on the southern slopes of BEAULNE spur, 9392.

At 1030 the attack opened with 1 Kings on the east of the canal and R. Berks west of it, the detachments K.R.R.C. moving along the spurs on either side. The R. Berks outstripped 1 Kings, who, in turn, outstripped the detachment of K.R.R.C. on their right. The R. Berks gained the slopes of the small spur N.E. of BRAYE by 1200 hrs. The 1 Kings advanced somewhat later almost to the foot of the main ridge where they were checked by fire from the front, and from their right flank and rear, the two Coys. K.R.R.C. having been driven back to the end of the BEAULNE spur by a counter-attack. An effort was made with the help of 2 Worcs. (5 Inf. Bde.) to clear the Germans from their enfilading positions but without success, and eventually the Kings and R. Berks had to withdraw. A line running roughly east and west a little to the north of FM. DE METZ 9292 was established about 1400 hrs.

The right detachment of K.R.R.C. meanwhile had been reinforced by 2 Worcs. and 2 H.L.I. (5 Inf. Bde.). These troops, supported on the right by 3 Inf. Bde., were able to stem the German attacks and hold a line a little forward of the right of 1 Kings.

The western two companies, K.R.R.C. on LA BOVETTE spur, 9192, edged off left-handed in the woods and at about 1400 hrs. came up on the right of 4 Guards Bde.

6 Inf. Bde., under heavy shell fire, held to the position taken up but was unable to advance further when a general advance was ordered in the evening.

12. Brig.-Gen. Haking with 2 Worcs. and 2 H.L.I. of his 5 Inf. Bde. and the two companies K.R.R.C. at about 1630 hrs. advanced up the BEAULNE spur. The advance continued in the dusk and reached the CHEMIN DE DAMES, but after sending out patrols right and left and finding only enemy, Haking considered it unwise to stay there unsupported. He accordingly withdrew to the south end of the BEAULNE spur.

13. 4 Guards Bde. were delayed at the start and it was not until 0830 hrs. that 2 Gren. Gds. crossed and moved towards SOUPIR. The rest of the brigade were not over until 1000 hrs.

In the meantime Major Sarsfield commanding 2 Conn. Rangers in SOUPIR, having heard at 0100 hrs. the line of advance of 4 Guards Bde., on his own initiative occupied COUR DE SOUPIR, 9091, about 0530 hrs. He pushed out small posts to CROIX SANS TETE, 9093, and to the flanks. No enemy was seen and the remainder of the battalion remained concentrated at COUR DE SOUPIR.

At 0945 hrs. the leading platoon of 2 Gren. Gds. arrived. Soo after the enemy were reported advancing. Three companies Conn. Rangers were hastily deployed east and west of the farm. The Germans attacked with two or three battalions supported by artillery and machine guns. As they came up the companies of 2 Gren. Gds. (Jeffreys) were put in on the left of the Conn. Rangers. The Germans made progress on the right and were within 100 yards of the farm when the 3 Coldm. Gds. (Matheson) arrived about 1020 hrs. and brought the enemy advance to a halt. The I. G., when they in turn came up, were sent to clear the woods on the right.

Matheson and Jeffreys arranged for an attack with their two battalions. The attack started at 1200 hrs. but was thrown into confusion by Germans surrendering, as, while the prisoners were being collected, fire was opened by fresh enemy troops.

Another attack was made by the I. G. on the right at about 1400 hrs. but it was checked on leaving the woods. About this time the K.R.R.C. detachment came up on the extreme right.

About 1600 hrs. the line was stabilized from LA BOVETTE in front of COUR DE SOUPIR along the edge of the spur towards CHAVONNE. Two Companies, 2 Coldm. Gds. were sent to CHAVONNE where they got in touch with 1 Cav. Bde. later. The other two companies went in support of the I. G. and made touch with the K.R.R.C. about 1630 hrs.

4 Guards Bde. were too disorganized to take part in the advance ordered in the evening, though there was some forward movement in the woods on the right. A counter-attack was repulsed by rifle and machine gun fire aided by a section of 18 prs., which had come up during the afternoon. This was the only artillery support the brigade had all day.

14. About 1400 hrs. Haig heard of the repulse of 3 Div., and realized his left flank was in danger. He sent 1 and 2 Cav. Bdes. to CHAVONNE and SOUPIR. 1 Cav. Bde. arrived at CHAVONNE at 1530 hrs. The only battalion in corps reserve was 1 Oxf. Bucks. at SOUPIR.

15. **Artillery, 2 Div.—14 Sep.**
   (a) 34 Bde. R.F.A. with 6 Inf. Bde.
       All batteries supported the advance on BRAYE. 50 Bty., supporting R. Berks., whose commander paid periodical visits to the O.P., fired steadily all day. The brigade had many casualties to men and horses.
   (b) 36 Bde. R.F.A. with 4 Gds. Bde.
       Had great difficulty in finding positions. Only one forward section fired.
   (c) 41 Bde. R.F.A. crossed at BOURG and later re-crossed and took up a position above VIEIL ARCY. Only fired 12 rounds at the enemy attacking 4 Guards Bde.

(d) 44 (How.) Bde. R.F.A. came into action near VERNEUIL but fired little or nothing.

(e) 35 Hy. Bty. in action in a poor position west of BOURG. One section sent back to heights above VIEIL ARCY. The battery only fired 34 rounds all day.

Stand No. 7.

A point just east of the bend in the road above TROYON, 972943.

Operations of 1 Div.—14 Sep.

1. At 0300 hrs., in heavy rain and mist, 2 Inf. Bde. moved by VENDRESSE on TROYON, 2 K.R.R.C. leading, followed by 2 R. Sussex, which was to remain in VENDRESSE until needed. K.R.R.C. occupied TROYON about 0400 hrs. and the leading company went on to the top of the hill. After surprising a German piquet, about 0445 hrs., it was checked and the remainder of the K.R.R.C. extended the line. Though there was an absence of artillery fire, rifle fire was now intense. By 0630 hrs. 2 R. Sussex were deployed on the left of K.R.R.C., and about this time the Northants were sent to the next spur to the east.

The R. Sussex, by moving two companies round to the west, were able to take the German trenches in the flank. After a sharp fire fight the Germans surrendered and, progressing further, the R. Sussex were able to get their machine gun section into the SUCRERIE and enfilade the enemy opposing the K.R.R.C. to the east. More Germans surrendered and a battery entrenched east of the SUCRERIE opened fire on friend and foe alike, but the German gunners, and the teams that came up, were shot down.

It was now about 0700 hrs. and the head of 1 Guards Bde. had arrived at VENDRESSE; 3 Inf. Bde. (less 1 Queens, which was on its way to PAISSY plateau to act as flank guard) was in reserve at MOULINS. 1 and 4 Cav. Bdes. were waiting near PAISSY and 2 Cav. Bde. about VENDRESSE.

Between 0800 and 0900 hrs. the battle became intense. The Loyals went up in support of the R. Sussex and K.R.R.C., and with Northants working forward on the right, 2 Inf. Bde. advanced and took up a position on the flat top of the ridge, north of the CHEMIN DES DAMES, where they entrenched.

2. Meanwhile 1 Guards Bde. was moving up on the left of 2 Inf. Bde. 1 Coldm. Gds. were sent through the woods on the TROYON spur to come in on the left of R. Sussex, the Camerons and Black Watch were to find a way on to the south-west end of TROYON spur on the left of the Coldm. Gds.

Soon after 0800 hrs. 1 Coldm. Gds. reached the top of the spur and found the Camerons and Black Watch already there. Together with the Camerons on their left 1 Coldm. Gds. attacked on the left of R. Sussex. They were met by heavy fire and both battalions suffered severely. They eventually reached the CHEMIN DES

DAMES road where, owing to the lack of cover, they continued to lose heavily.

The remainder of the operations of 1 Guards Bde. and 2 Inf. Bde. is described under Stand No. 8.

3. About 1000 hrs. the divisional commander ordered 3 Inf. Bde. to reinforce the left of 1 Guards Bde., to gain the CHEMIN DES DAMES above CHIVY and link up with 2 Div. on the left. At this time the brigade only had 1 S.W.B., 2 Welch and two Coys. 1 Glosters, the other two companies being in divisional reserve. The S.W.B. and Welch had just deployed across the CHIVY valley, when about 1030 hrs. the German 25 Res. Bde. advanced south-west with its right on CHIVY. The fog had just lifted and the attack was met by fire from 3 Inf. Bde. and two Fd. Btys. and broke down, 3 Inf. Bde. establishing themselves on the south-east slopes of the BEAULNE spur.

Stand No. 8.

CHEMIN DES DAMES south of CERNY, about 974946.

Operations of 1 Div.—14 Sep. continued.

1. About 0900 hrs. 2 Inf. Bde. had started to entrench roughly on the line of the CHEMIN DES DAMES and shortly after 1 Coldm. Gds. had aligned itself on the left under heavy fire. Col. Ponsonby, commanding 1 Coldm. Gds., collected the equivalent of a company and led them forward to the village of CERNY and later to a wood beyond. The situation was very obscure owing to the fog. This party remained isolated during the day but caused the enemy many casualties by rifle fire. In the meantime the rest of 1 Coldm. Gds. worked eastwards under the crest and took up a position on the right of the K.R.R.C.

2. Further to the east 1 Queens, the right flank guard, also crossed the CHEMIN DES DAMES and met with no serious resistance until it reached the northern slope about LA BOVELLE FE, 9895. Here the battalion took up a position and engaged the enemy north of the AILETTE by rifle and machine gun fire.

3. At 1300 hrs. the Germans launched another counter-attack on the entire front of 1 Guards Bde. and 2 Inf. Bde. This drove the R. Sussex south of the SUCRERIE and exposed the right of the Camerons, who were driven back with heavy loss into the CHIVY valley. The two Coys. of 1 Glosters with the 3 Inf. Bde. were sent forward and the line was stabilized. The situation remained practically unchanged until 1500 hrs. The Germans continued to put in attacks but they gradually became weaker. By this time the whole of the infantry of 1 Div. had been engaged except the two companies in divisional reserve.

4. At 1630, as the German attacks had died down, Haig ordered a general advance. The light was failing fast before 1 Div. was

under way. The only appreciable progress was made by 3 Inf. Bde., who got forward to within 300 yards of the CHEMIN DES DAMES just short of the SUCRERIE. The brigade was never in touch with 5 Inf. Bde., which attacked up the BEAULNE spur about the same time.

5. During the afternoon the position of 1 Queens became more precarious owing to the French being beaten back on the right. By 1630 hrs. the battalion commander had withdrawn to the right of the line on the CHEMIN DES DAMES.

The detachment of Coldm. Gds. at CERNY started back about midnight guided by an officer with a compass. Progress was slow as the colonel, who was wounded, had to be carried most of the way. They eventually arrived near VENDRESSE sometime before daylight.

6. Artillery 1 Div.—14 Sep.

The mist handicapped the artillery on both sides until nearly noon.

(a) 116 Bty. with 1 Gds. Bde. came into action west of TROYON about 1100 hrs. almost in the front line.

(b) 25 Bde. R.F.A. (less 115 Bty.) with 2 Inf. Bde.

114 Bty. in action at 1100 hrs. east of TROYON.

113 Bty. was on the road just south of CHIVY and in action about 1100 hrs. It fired on the attack of 25 Res. Bde. with deadly effect, and continued to support 3 Inf. Bde.

(c) 39 Fd. Bde. with 3 Inf. Bde.

54 Bty. first in action west of VENDRESSE but had to move to a position $\frac{1}{2}$ mile north of MOULINS, where it did excellent work in support of 2 Inf. Bde.

46 Bty. came into action near 113 Bty. and covered 3 Inf. Bde. and helped to repulse the counter-attack.

51 Bty. in action south of the road MOULINS—VENDRESSE sent a section to TROYON spur, where it was under voice control. It had many good targets and knocked out several enemy guns.

(d) The remainder were ordered to be in readiness west of JUMIGNY 0091 to support the advance.

26 Bde. R.F.A. (less 116 Bty.) was in close support of 1 Queens.

117 and 118 Btys. were in action nearly up to the CHEMIN DES DAMES soon after 1030 hrs.

115 Bty. (25 Bde. R.F.A.) was near ARBRE DE PAISSY 0093 during the morning but did not fire. About 1600 hrs. it came into action in a gravel pit on northern edge of the TROYON spur and engaged the counter-attack down the CHIVY valley.

(e) 43 (How.) Bde.

30 and 57 Btys., in support of 1 Queens, were in action about 1200 hrs. on the PAISSY plateau a little behind 113 and 117 Btys. They had good targets at short range during the counter-attacks in the afternoon.

40 Bty. was sent by the C.R.A. to support the left of the division and came into action near 46 Bty.

The batteries supporting 1 Queens had to move back when the latter retired. This they did, covered by a section each of 118 and 30 Btys., which remained in action until dark.

(f) 26 Hy. Bty. had one section in action near ARBRE DE PAISSY and another about TOUR DE PAISSY 9991.

(g) Owing to the thick mist in the morning up till almost mid-day the artillery could do nothing. As will have been gathered, brigades were mixed up and batteries often widely separated. This was due in some measure to the mist but more to the piecemeal attacks, which were the result of the belief that the advance would continue. Battery commanders were in consequence very much on their own.

7. I Corps—15 Sep.

This was a day of sorting out units and of improving the positions gained. There were a few minor German attacks, which were repulsed without difficulty, and some shelling.

Thus ended the battle of the AISNE. The Allied effort had failed and German XVIII Corps had arrived in addition to the VII Reserve, XV and XII Corps. The chances of success by frontal attack were past, the only flank open was on the east and on that flank only the chances of a decision rested. Trench warfare on the battle front had begun and the race to the sea was started.

V

PRINCIPAL LESSONS OF THE BATTLE.

1. Appreciation of the situation and plan.

The extract from the Official History given on page 47 and our post-war knowledge of events makes it clear how exceedingly difficult it is for a commander to pierce the fog of war in order to arrive at correct appreciations of ever-changing developments in the situations. The fact remains that, if G.H.Q. had appreciated that the situation on the nights of 11 and 12 Sep. and that on the night of 13 Sep. were entirely different—that on the former dates time was all essential in order to forestall the enemy on the CHEMIN DES DAMES—that in the latter case the race was lost and a highly co-ordinated plan was vital to success—and if the plan and will of the C.-in-C. had been impressed upon his subordinates, the battle of the AISNE would undoubtedly have assumed an entirely different shape favourable to the Allies.

2. The necessity for orders to make the intention unmistakable to the recipients.

None of the G.H.Q. orders at this period disclose the intention of the C.-in-C.

The fact that roads were allotted and pursuit was indicated had the inevitable effect that, on both 13th and 14th, formations started off in column of route covered by advanced guards, and consequently blundered into action piecemeal, *e.g.*, 5 Div., which had to alter its plan and attack CHIVRES spur; 6 Inf. Bde., which marched up the BRAYE valley with a battalion as advanced guard, and with flank guards; 1 Div., which endeavoured to get into column of route on one road when it was suitably placed for an advance on a two brigade front.

3. The influence of the personality of a commander.

The influence of Brig.-Gen. Hunter-Weston made possible the exploit of 11 Inf. Bde. on the night 12/13. Everybody was tired, wet and hungry and yet he led them several miles over difficult roads and finally launched the battalions on a steep climb against an enemy of unknown strength (*vide* Part VI).

4. The tasks which well disciplined troops of high morale can accomplish.

The B.E.F. had been marching and fighting, except for two days' rest, ever since it left its concentration area. The weather had been bad for the previous few days; boots and clothing were wearing out. The performance of 11 Inf. Bde. on the night 12/13 was typical.

5. The night advance. (F.S.R., Vol. II, 1929, Sec. 97.)

The advance of 11 Inf. Bde. by night gained a position that would have otherwise only been obtained by hard fighting. Consideration of the move of the Conn. Rangers to COUR DE SOUPIR gives rise to the question as to how the operations of 2 Div. would have been affected had 5 Inf. Bde. secured a firm footing on the BEAULNE and SOUPIR spurs on the night of 13/14, and part at least of the rest of the division moved over the river. This would have saved more than four hours on the morning of 14th, and enabled the advance of I Corps to have been co-ordinated.

If the other bridges could have been seized during the night 12/13, it would have greatly facilitated the advance on 13th.

6. **Touch with the enemy should not be lost.** (F.S.R., Vol. II, 1929, Sec. 30, 6.)

There was no reconnaissance to speak of on the front of I Corps on the night of 13/14. Owing to lack of information early on 14th, which should have been forthcoming had patrols been sent out, the advanced guards of both divisions were forced to deploy, in the confusion of surprise, from the cramped valleys about TROYON and LA MAISON BRULEE respectively, and found themselves crowded on to ground too restricted for their proper employment and in complete ignorance of their surroundings.

7. **The principle of concentration and use of reserves.**

The B.E.F. advanced to the AISNE with its divisions spread over the front and all were committed to the battle on 13th. There was no reserve except 19 Inf. Bde. on the extreme left. No effort was made by G.H.Q. to concentrate superior force against the gap in the German line, and, having no reserve, G.H.Q. were unable on 13th or 14th to reinforce I Corps front, where alone there was room north of the AISNE for manœuvre and for artillery positions to support a further advance.

During 14th I Corps' local reserves were thrown into the fight where the enemy resistance was strongest (*cf.* F.S.R., Vol. II, 1929, Sec. 64, 8). No troops were available to exploit the advance of the Queens and the corps commander had no reserve to put in when he ordered the general advance late in the afternoon.

8. **The principle of co-operation.**

Co-operation in this battle was confined generally to that fortuitously arranged by commanders on the spot. There was little co-ordination in attacks between adjacent brigades and none between divisions. The lack of communications no doubt had a great deal to do with it. The co-operation between the artillery and infantry was limited to those cases where battery positions were near the troops supported. It must be remembered that the idea of a fire plan as we now know it was unheard of in 1914, and the artillery were expected to co-operate in an infantry attack as best they could.

9. **The use of mobile troops.**

The cavalry were allotted no definite role either during the approach to the AISNE on 12th or during the battle. No doubt men and horses were tired but Cav. Bdes. only marched 10-14 miles on 12th. In addition to attempting to seize the crossings that night, it appears that they could have been usefully employed on 13th and 14th to exploit the situation on the right.

10. **" To launch infantry to the attack without adequate covering fire will result only in unnecessary casualties."** (I.T., Vol. II, 1931, Sec. 10, 5.)

The attacks of 5 Div. on CHIVRES spur were a typical example among the many that could be quoted.

11. **Economy of force.**

On 14th, 5 Div. attacked CHIVRES spur with 9 battalions (admittedly depleted) on a front of 2,500 yards, with the result that they tended to close in on the centre, leading to confusion and heavy loss.

In the fighting round the SUCRERIE on a frontage of less than a mile the greater part of two infantry brigades was engaged.

12. **The influence of ground as affecting the siting of artillery** (*see* diagram in pocket at end).

With the range of the 1914 18-pr. gun, the nature of the ground made the task of the artillery of the B.E.F. particularly difficult. It was almost impossible to give adequate support to the infantry owing to the width of the valley. O.Ps. on the south side of the river were too far away to ensure close support, and the difficulty of employing forward observation at such long ranges with insufficient cable and telephones was very great. I Div. had not these difficulties, neither had 5 Div. opposite CHIVRES, where observation from the plateau south of the river was much closer and good.

Great as were the technical difficulties, they were not entirely insuperable, nor can the inadequate support afforded by the artillery be attributed solely to this cause. The failure was due far more to the faulty tactical teaching of 1914 in regard to the attack, and to the system of organization, whereby the whole of the artillery was decentralized to divisions; it did not even stop at divisions.

F.S.R., Vol. II, 1929, Sec. 63, 5, was as true in 1914 as it is to-day; yet, in this battle, the tactics invariably employed were to launch the infantry to the attack in the place and at the time best suited to the infantry and to ask the artillery, as an afterthought, to co-operate as best it could.

Up to mid-day on 14th an attack on I Corps front and on the front of 5 Div. would have succeeded had any attempt been made to concentrate the fire of the bulk of the artillery in support of it.

It was not realized in 1914 that artillery must be handled in battle like other arms in accordance with the principle of " Economy of force " and concentration at the decisive point, and that it is by concentration of *fire power* rather than of *men* at the decisive point that successful attack is made possible.

13. **Surprise.**

The employment by the Germans of howitzers of large calibre constituted a form of surprise.

14. **The choice and occupation of the defensive position by the Germans.**

The great natural strength of the position needs no emphasis.

It is possible that, if the Germans had held the actual line of the river in any strength, the British would have been unable to force the passage frontally (but our artillery would have had a better chance of bringing effective fire to bear on the enemy infantry) without considerable delay, during which the enemy would have had ample time further to consolidate his defence in the CHEMIN DES DAMES area.

The Germans have explained that their peace time teaching required one single strong line and a long field of fire, and that they went back to the top of the plateau to secure these.

The advantages of depth in a defensive position would have been recognized by them to-day. The lack of depth between the CHEMIN DES DAMES ridge and the AILLETTE valley would therefore have led them to organize their position in depth from the AISNE.

VI

THE UNCONQUERABLE MIND

A STUDY OF A NIGHT OPERATION

By " B. Buckley."*

Reproduced from the Journal of the Royal United Services Institution by kind permission of the Editor.

The special responsibility of commanders and staffs in connection with night operations is to ensure that :—
  i. *the plan is simple ;*
  ii. *thorough reconnaissance by day and, if practicable, by night is carried out. All arrangements . . . must be worked out with the utmost care."*—F.S.R., Vol. II, Sec. 97, 1.

" *The principal duty of a commander is to make decisions . . . In war, a commander may find that his attention tends to be distracted by physical fatigue, his mind to be inspired with misgiving . . . ; if he possesses the essential attributes of command, he will remain unshaken, and by his knowledge and determination will compel the attainment of his object."*—F.S.R., Vol. II, 1929, Sec. 5, 2.

In peace there appears to be a tendency to place an undue value on the technique of war at the expense of a proper appreciation of its psychology. Yet, technique or no technique, it is the spirit of the commander which has so often in the past turned, and will again in the future turn, the balance between success and failure.

Although, where exercises are well conducted, one sees attempts made to keep the solutions on " practical " lines, and to discount any system which classifies solutions with regard to the nearness of

---

* The author acknowledges, with thanks, assistance from many sources.

their approach to the requirements of the manual, nevertheless the manual remains, in effect, the criterion by which all are judged. Indeed it is difficult to see how this can be avoided. One cannot say to a hypothetical " Smith " :—" Your solution is good, inasmuch as it is practical and violates no principles of war nor any of the instructions of the manual. Nevertheless you can receive no credit for it, for your psychology is such that you are not capable of making such a decision in war, much less of putting it into effect." For, apart from the more obvious objection, " Smith's " psychology may be such as to make the words of peace more difficult than the deeds of war.

This being so, it is mildly surprising to find how little the psychological aspect, admittedly difficult to test, is glossed over in the use which is made of a study of military history. If we may not test, surely we should study. Apart from that type of study of military history which may conveniently be designated " narrative " history, which is usually of more interest than value, and which calls not so much for a student of war as for a reader of history, we are encouraged to concentrate on campaigns, and on incidents in them, which show the evil of disregarding the instructions of the regulations, and the good which follows adherence to their precepts. Not infrequently thoughts and reasoning are attributed to long-dead captains of the military art which one has difficulty in believing could have all occurred to any but a superman. And, while all this tends to glorify the book, it does not go to the root of the matter, which is the man—not his manual.

Now while it is not the intention of the author to belittle the importance of military text-books, nor, indeed, to decry their necessity, it is suggested that, from time to time, military history might be made to serve the purpose of rectifying the balance between the relative importance of psychology and the technique of war ; that we might with advantage study, not read, some action in which the manual is transgressed and replaced by the unconquerable mind of the commander. Such an action is that of the 11th Infantry Brigade of the 4th Division, III Corps, on the night of 12th-13th September, 1914, and this is a rough outline of what happened. It is a story of a night operation, and, when the student has read and grasped its essential features, he should turn to the manual to find the technical lessons, and to himself for the other—and main— lesson of this incident.

It will be recalled that the first troops to cross the AISNE from south to north in September, 1914, were those of the 11th Infantry Brigade. Sir John French's plans for the advance on 12th September included the crossing of that river. The III Corps had been directed upon the ridge at VENIZEL.* By about 3 p.m. the Divisional Cavalry had reached the heights overlooking the river,

---

* For the full narrative of the crossing see Official History, 1914, 3rd Edition, p. 379 and Maps 34 and 35.

while the leading infantry, the 12th Infantry Brigade, had reached SEPTMONTS. At that time the Germans were still occupying the southern bank.

At nightfall the situation was that on the right of the III Corps were the 3rd and 5th Cavalry Brigades in an area which excluded VAILLY, but included CHASSEMY—CIRY—SALSOGNE—CONDE SUR AISNE. The II Corps was behind the cavalry in an area which included BRENELLE — BRAINE — CHACRISE — SERCHES. The relevant portions of the III Corps itself were disposed as follows: the 12th Infantry Brigade, finding the advanced guard and subsequently the outposts, was about VENIZEL—BILLY SUR AISNE with reserve at ACY; the 11th infantry Brigade was at SEPTMONTS, with the 10th and 19th Infantry Brigades behind it at BUZANCY; the 31st (Heavy) and 28th (Field) Batteries were in position east of SEPTMONTS. On the left of the III Corps the French 43rd Division were in and about SOISSONS.

Before dark the advanced guard—12th Infantry Brigade—now finding outposts, had pushed two companies forward into the village of VENIZEL and, as a result of this advance, the Germans had attempted to blow up the bridge and had retired to trenches on the northern bank. The brigade had at this time covered some eighteen to twenty miles in rain over muddy roads; it had twice deployed, and the troops were wet through, tired and hungry, having had no food since 5 a.m.—nor was any food now available. Such little information as was to hand tended to show that the Germans were continuing their retirement. The outpost commander had reported that the bridge at VENIZEL had not been destroyed by the retreating enemy, but was only damaged. It was still capable of taking both infantry and cavalry in file, but it was commanded by trenches on the northern bank. As far as was known, all the other bridges over the AISNE were impassable, except that at CONDÉ, which was strongly held.

At VENIZEL the AISNE is some sixty yards broad and unfordable. At this point the river wanders to the south side of the valley and passes under the steep slopes of the southern heights. To the north, stretch the flat and open meadow lands of the valley itself, devoid of cover, and for the mile and a half of its breadth commanded by the BUCY LE LONG spur, which forms the skyline. A single road leads from VENIZEL to BUCY, with numerous tracks and paths branching from it to the east and north-east. The general conformation of the ground was such as to deny to us artillery positions on the south side of the river from which we could effectively reply to the enemy guns which covered the valley at short range from the northern heights.

So much for a brief description of the scene of action. When we come to study the action itself, it will be found to embrace every feature of a night operations from reconnaissance to consolidation.

Its execution, especially in view of the condition of the troops at the time, must make the manual shudder. About 5 p.m. on 12th, the exhausted battalions of the 11th Infantry Brigade were ordered to halt and obtain food in SEPTMONTS, preparatory to pushing on to seize the crossing at VENIZEL that night. As we have seen eighteen miles had already been covered, through mud and rain, in the face of an active and unbeaten enemy, and for the younger generation which has not yet experienced the moral and physical effects of prolonged operations in the field, it is, perhaps, difficult if not impossible to appreciate the cumulative results of bad weather, bullets, and a shortage of food : the first and last have often been too much for many of us, even in peace. On this night SEPTMONTS yielded but little to eat, but the halt was welcome.

The brigade commander had already been down to VENIZEL on the back of a motor-cycle. He now sent out a reconnaissance party. One officer was responsible for reconnoitring the route forward to the bridge and, on return, was to guide the column. Another was to ascertain the condition of the bridge and report. A third was to remain in observation of the crossing and to endeavour to find out if the trenches opposite to it were held. A local guide was provided, but subsequently lost. This reconnaissance, therefore, covered the stage of the night march only—here the manual stirs uneasily !

At about 9.30 p.m. the bridge was reported passable by infantry in single file at two paces distance. An hour later the column started with the brigade commander acting as guide, the officer detailed for that duty being at that time unavailable. Towards midnight of 12th/13th September, the column reached VENIZEL, having covered some three miles in ninety minutes in continuation of the full day's march which had brought it earlier in the day to SEPTMONTS. On arrival at the village, the officer who had remained at the bridge reported that the enemy appeared to have withdrawn. Some idea of the weather conditions under which the march had been carried out may be gathered from an unusually descriptive extract from a war diary : " amid sheets of rain and a howling gale the exhausted troops, without food since 5 a.m., to whom extra ammunition had been issued at SEPTMONTS, staggered over the hill and the three miles to VENIZEL, not caring whither or why they went, driven on by the determination of their commander." Here indeed had mind conquered mind, that mind might conquer matter.

While the main body of the brigade remained halted in the village, its advanced guard, finding the trenches on the northern bank empty, filed across the bridge and formed a covering party just beyond it. As soon as this bridge-head had been formed, the remainder of the brigade crossed over and assembled on the northern bank in mass. This movement was controlled by officers at the bridge, the troops being guided to their positions on the other side of the river. By 2 a.m. on 13th the crossing was completed.

During the time that the brigade was in process of assembly the brigade commander issued orders personally to an officer detailed by one of the battalions to take a patrol out to "the right hill," meaning the one north of STE. MARGUERITE : this patrol turns up again later on in the story. In order to hold the crossing which had been effected, it was, in the opinion of the brigade commander, necessary to occupy the high ground above BUCY LE LONG. While the brigade was being assembled on the northern bank, he called a conference of battalion and company commanders and issued some such verbal orders as these : " the enemy were seen retreating from SOISSONS in the evening, and I expect their rear guards are on the heights above BUCY LE LONG. I intend to gain a footing on these heights to cover the passage of the 4th Division to-morrow. In an hour's time you will see three spurs faintly against the sky. The right spur will be taken with the bayonet by the 1st Rifle Brigade, the centre by the 1st Hampshires, the left by the 1st Somerset. The East Lancashires will be in reserve behind the centre. Each battalion will send out an officer's patrol to the spur it is to capture. There is to be no firing."

Here, I think, the manual finds itself on the horns of a dilemma, torn between appreciation of simplicity and disapproval of omissions of what it has stated to be essentials. Let the student detect these omissions, and in doing so bear in mind the circumstances in which these orders were issued. Possibly his investigations may lead him to the conclusion that extreme simplicity is more easily digested food for tired men than the elaborate diet prescribed by military technique, a diet which, in circumstances much less exacting than these, might well lead to mental nausea.

At 3.30 a.m. battalions moved off independently to start a night advance of some two and a half miles, to be followed by a night attack up slopes which might, for these tired men, with truth be described as precipices. The brigade had not waited for the return of its officer's patrol and had, therefore, moved in entire ignorance of what was in front of it. The formation in general use was column of route with an advanced guard of one company about fifty yards ahead of the main body.

Shortly after moving off, the advanced guard of one battalion encountered some men moving towards it, and an order to charge was given. At that moment, however, the rustle and squelch of the advancing column was momentarily drowned by the sound of a heavy fall and a volley of oaths. The "enemy" recognizing the familiar words, succeeded in countermanding their opponents' order to charge. The patrol had rejoined ! It reported having moved out on the main VENIZEL—BUCY road and then struck out half-right along one of the numerous tracks which exist in that part of the valley. On reaching the BUCY—CONDÉ road it had turned right-handed and had proceeded in the direction of STE. MARGUERITE until it met a road block, probably just east of

LE MONCEL. Anticipating that the enemy were in a position to bring fire to bear on the obstacle, it was decided that the role of the patrol was best fulfilled by returning to guide its battalion to this point, rather than by continuing a reconnaissance which might alarm the enemy and give warning of the main advance. It had therefore withdrawn.

The student may well pause here, and quivering manual in hand, reflect upon night patrols in general and on this one in particular.

Just before daylight the steep slopes of the ridge came into sight. The troops deployed and started to scramble upwards. As day dawned, the crest was reached without opposition, and patrols went forward to gain touch with the Germans. Shortly afterwards orders were received that no further advance was to take place, and here, with the arrival of daylight, we may leave the study of this omnibus night operation.

It may be said that to extract lessons from an action in which everything went well when, according to the book, everything should have gone wrong, is an unusual task for a student of military history. It ought not to be unusual, for it will often be profitable. In the author's solution to the task there are six main lessons of military technique. They are not difficult to find. The harder road is the road of the real lesson of this little incident in a huge campaign, and it is to be found in each individual's answer to two questions :—

Firstly—as commander of this brigade in these circumstances, what would I have done; what would I have been capable of doing ?

Secondly—what is there in this action which may be held to account for its success; was it something which, by its absence, was responsible for such a failure as that on " RHODODENDRON RIDGE " (ANZAC) on a night in August, 1915; and does our training, in any way, recognize such factors ?

VII

RETROSPECT OF THE BATTLE

(Extract from " Military Operations, France and Belgium, Volume I, 1914, pp. 465-457.)

Thus ended for the British the fighting on the AISNE in 1914; and the narrative may be closed with a very brief review of the battle.

The disappointing results of the operations on 12th/14th September, after which a deadlock ensued, seem to have been due to a failure of the High Command to appreciate the situation, and exploit the still existing gap in the enemy's line. It was at any rate partly due to the neglect to exercise control and issue orders which would have made the essential requirements of the situation clear to subordinate commanders.

The forcing of the AISNE was likely to involve a race with hostile reinforcements, in which the Germans had the advantage, as they were falling back. This race was lost mainly owing to the failure to make a resolute effort even to reconnoitre the enemy's dispositions on the river, and, except in the 4th Division, to push forward parties to seize the bridges on the night of 12th/13th. On 13th, when the divisions made a rather cautious and leisurely advance, they should have been reminded, in spite of their fatigue after over three weeks' continuous operations, that "sweat saves blood." In the G.H.Q. orders there was no hint whatever of the importance of time.

By the evening of 13th September, the situation had completely changed. German reinforcements were known to have arrived, and serious resistance was to be expected on 14th; yet the G.H.Q. orders merely repeated the formula that "the Army will continue the pursuit . . . and act vigorously against the retreating enemy"; they gave no more tactical direction than to allot roads. There was no plan, no objective, no arrangements for co-operation, and the divisions blundered into battle.

The actual passage of the AISNE is likely to be remembered in the annals of the Army as a very remarkable feat; for it involved forcing a passage frontally without possibility of manœuvre. The Germans excuse their failure to stop the British at the river line by the explanation that their peace-time teaching required one single strong line and a long field of fire, and that to secure these they went back to the top of the plateau. The advance of the 11th Brigade alone across the damaged bridge at VENIZEL was a most audacious move; yet at no point did the crossing of any one body of troops facilitate the passage of others, owing to the topography of the valley and the small depth of the position gained on the north side of the river. But for the German failure to destroy the aqueduct at BOURG completely, it is possible that the British might have been unable to maintain their firm hold on the north bank. By way of that aqueduct, however, the guns of the 1st Division managed to cross the river and find effective positions at once. Thus Sir Douglas Haig, taking instant advantage of his opportunity, was able to make his bold thrust forward on 14th and to establish his right on the CHEMIN DES DAMES, where his troops clung to the shallow holes which did duty for trenches, with a tenacity beyond all praise. For want of another division in reserve, he was unable to push his advance further; to the west of TROYON the 2nd Division, the II Corps and the III Corps were pinned to their ground and could give him no help.

Regarding the AISNE in the light of the ditch of a fortress only the I Corps had really passed over it and could see any prospect of carrying forward its attack. The II and III Corps had practically made no more than a lodgment on the escarp,* above which they dared not show their heads. They could find no effective positions for their artillery; and for a time could make little reply to the German bombardment except with rifle fire. Indeed, had not the enemy frequently assaulted the British lines in force and in close formation, the British would have had little to show in return for the casualties which they suffered from the German artillery. As matters fell out, the Germans gave on many occasions the very opportunity of which the British soldier could take advantage, and he did so to the full extent.

It is somewhat difficult to arrive at the total number of German formations which fought the British five, eventually six, divisions on the AISNE; for single brigades from many corps were put into the line. Thus we know that, apart from the cavalry and two heavy howitzer batteries, the British I Corps was opposed not only by the VII Reserve Corps, but by a mixed detachment of the XII Corps consisting of the 63rd Brigade, three batteries and a heavy howitzer battery; the 50th Brigade of the XVIII Corps; five battalions of the XV Corps, the 25th Landwehr Brigade, and 1,200 men of the X Corps; a total of over 20 extra battalions. The British II Corps had opposite it the German III Corps with the 34th Brigade of the IX Corps interposed between its divisions, and two heavy howitzer batteries, as well as, on at least one day, a regiment of VII Corps. The four infantry brigades of the III Corps had in front of them the German II Corps, whose front was from CHIVRES sector (exclusive) to CUFFIES. Thus recalling that German brigades contained six battalions to the British four, there were at least 100 German battalions to 78 British (including the 6th Division).

VIII

ORDER OF BATTLE OF TROOPS ENGAGED

B.E.F.

(a) *Cav. Div.* (Allenby.)

    1 Cav. Bde. (Briggs.)
        Bays. 5 D.G. 11 H.

    2 Cav. Bde. (de Lisle.)
        4 D.G. 9 L. 18 H.

    4 Cav. Bde. (Bingham.)
        Household Cav. 6 D.G. 3 H.

---

* The defender's side of the ditch of a fortress.

Div. Arty. (Drake).
   7 Bde., R.H.A. (Birch.)
      "I" Bty.†
   32 Bde. R.F.A. (detached from 4 Div).
Div. Engineers.
   1 Fd. Sqn., R.E.

(b) *Gough's Command.** (Gough.)

   3 Cav. Bde. (Vaughan.)
      4 H.   5 L.   16 L.
   5 Cav. Bde. (Chetwode.)
      Greys.   12 L.   20 H.
   3 Bde., R.H.A. (Breeks.)
      "D" and "E" Btys.
   "J" Bty., R.H.A.
   4 Fd. Tp., R.E.

(c) 1 *Corps.* (Haig.)

   B.G.R.A. (Horne.)
   1 *Div.* (Lomax.)

      1 Guards Bde. (Maxse.)
         1 Coldm. Gds.   1 S.G.   1 Camerons.   1 Black Watch.
      2 Inf. Bde. (Bulfin.)
         2 R. Sussex.   1 Loyals.   1 Northamptons.
         2 K.R.R.C.
      3 Inf. Bde. (Landon.)
         1 Queen's.   1 S.W.B.   1 Glosters.   2 Welch.
      "A" Sqn., 15 H.

      Div. Arty.

         25 Bde., R.F.A.
            113, 114, 115 Btys.
         26 Bde., R.F.A.
            116, 117, 118 Btys.
         39 Bde., R.F.A.
            46, 51, 54 Btys.
         43 (How.) Bde., R.F.A.
            30, 40, 57 How. Btys.
         26 Hy. Bty., R.G.A.
      Div. Engineers. (Schreiber.)
         23 and 26 Fd. Coys., R.E.

---

† "L" Battery, which belonged to the 7th Bde. R.H.A., was cut up at NERY on 1 Sep., and was replaced later by "H" Battery from home.

* From 6 Sep. the 3rd and 5th Cavalry Brigades acted together under Brigadier-General Hubert Gough. On 16 Sep. this force was officially designated the 2nd Cavalry Division.

2 *Div.* (Monro.)
- 4 Guards Bde. (Feilding.)
    - 2 Gren. Gds. 2 Coldm. Gds. 3 Coldm. Gds. 1 I.G.
- 5 Inf. Bde. (Haking.)
    - 2 Worcesters. 2 Oxf. Bucks. 2 H.L.I. 2 Conn. Rangers.
- 6 Inf. Bde. (Davies (N.Z.).)
    - 1 Kings. 2 S. Staffords. 1 R. Berks. 1 K.R.R.C.
- "B" Sqn., 15 H.
- Div. Arty. (Perceval.)
    - 34 Bde., R.F.A.
        - 22, 50, 70 Btys.
    - 36 Bde., R.F.A.
        - 15, 48, 71 Btys.
    - 41 Bde., R.F.A.
        - 9, 16, 17 Btys.
    - 44 (How.) Bde., R.F.A.
        - 47, 56, 60 How. Btys.
    - 35 Hy. Bty., R.G.A.
- Div. Engineers. (Boys.)
    - 5 and 11 Fd. Coys., R.E.

(d) *II Corps.* (Smith-Dorrien.)

B.G.R.A. (Short.)

3 *Div.* (Hubert Hamilton.)
- 7 Inf. Bde. (McCracken.)
    - 3 Worcesters. 2 P.W.V. 1 Wilts. 2 R.Ir. Rifles
- 8 Inf. Bde. (Doran.)
    - 2 R.S. 2 R.Irish. 4 Mx. 1 Gordons.
- 9 Inf. Bde. (Shaw.)
    - 1 N.F. 4 R.F. 1 Lincolns. 1 R.S.F.
- "C" Sqn., 15 H.
- Div. Arty. (Wing.)
    - 23 Bde., R.F.A.
        - 107, 108, 109 Btys.
    - 40 Bde., R.F.A.
        - 6, 23, 49 Btys.
    - 42 Bde., R.F.A.
        - 29, 41, 45 Btys.
    - 30 (How.) Bde., R.F.A.
        - 128, 129, 130 (How.) Btys.
    - 48 Hy. Bty., R.G.A.
- Div. Engineers. (Wilson).
    - 56 and 57 Fd. Coys., R.E.

5 *Div.* (Fergusson.)
    13 Inf. Bde. (Cuthbert.)
        2 K.O.S.B. 2 D.W.R. 1 R.W.K. 2 K.O.Y.L.I.
    14 Inf. Bde. (Rolt.)
        2 Suffolk. 1 Surreys. 1 D.C.L.I. 2 Manch.
    15 Inf. Bde. (Gleichen.)
        1 Norfolk. 1 Bedfs. 1 Cheshire. 2 Dorset.
    " A " Sqn., 19 H.
    Div. Arty. (Headlam.)
        15 Bde., R.F.A.
            11, 52, 80 Btys.
        27 Bde., R.F.A.
            119, 120, 121 Btys.
        28 Bde., R.F.A.
            122, 123, 124 Btys.
        8 (How.) Bde., R.F.A.
            37, 61, 65 (How.) Btys.
        108 Hy. Bty., R.G.A.
    Div. Engineers. (Tulloch.)
        17 and 59 Fd. Coy., R.E.

(e) *III Corps.* (Pulteney.)
    B.G.R.A. (Phipps-Hornby.)
    4 *Div.* (Wilson.)
        10 Inf. Bde. (Haldane.)
        1 Warwick. 2 Seaforth. 1 R.Ir.F. 2 R. Dublin F.
        11 Inf. Bde. (Hunter-Weston.)
        1 Som. L.I. 1 E. Lan. R. 1 Hamps. 1 R.B.
        12 Inf. Bde. (Anley.)
        1 King's Own. 2 L.F. 2 Inniskg. 2 Essex.
    " B " Sqn., 19 H.
    Div. Arty. (Milne.)
        14 Bde., R.F.A.
            39, 68, 88 Btys.
        29 Bde., R.F.A.
            125, 126, 127 Btys.
        32 Bde., R.F.A.*
            27, 134, 135 Btys.
        37 (How.) Bde., R.F.A.
            31, 35, 55 (How.) Btys.
        31 Hy. Bty., R.G.A.
    Div. Engineers. (Jones.)
        7 and 9 Fd. Coys., R.E.
    19 Inf. Bde. (Drummond.) 2 R.W.F. 1 Cameronians.
        1 Mx. 2 A. & S.H.

---

* On 12 Sep. the 32 Bde., R.F.A., came under the orders of the Cavalry Division.

2. **French.**

On the right of the B.E.F. was the XVIII Corps of the French Fifth Army (Franchet d'Esperey). The Corps consisted of two divisions, of which the 35th Colonial Division was on the immediate right of the B.E.F.

On the left of the B.E.F. was the VI Corps of the French Sixth Army (Maunoury). The Corps consisted of three divisions, of which the 45th Division was on the immediate left of the B.E.F.

3. **German.** (From 13 to 15 Sep., 1914.)

  (a) *II Army Corps.* (Von Linsingen.)

    3rd Infantry Division (CROUY 7489—VREGNY 7891).

      3rd Field Artillery Brigade :—

        2nd Field Artillery Regiment. (6 field gun batteries.)

        38th Field Artillery Regiment. (3 field gun, 3 light field howitzer batteries.)

    4th Infantry Division (PASLY 7090—CROUY).

      4th Field Artillery Brigade :—

        17th Field Artillery Regiment. (3 field gun batteries, 3 light field howitzer batteries. From 13/15 Sep., 1914, however, the 1/17th formed the Corps Reserve.)

        53rd Field Artillery Regiment. (6 field gun batteries.)

    Corps Artillery.

      I Battalion 15th Foot Artillery Regiment. (4 heavy field howitzer 5·9 batteries : during the period the battalion was attached to the 4th Infantry Division and placed by the latter under the 4th Field Artillery Brigade.)

    Attached Army Artillery.

      II Battalion 4th Foot Artillery Regiment. (Two 21-cm. mortar batteries : during the night of 13/14 Sep., the battalion took up its position.)

      II Battalion, 9th Reserve Foot Artillery Regiment. (Two 10-cm. gun batteries. On the morning of 14 Sep., the half battalion went into position, but on the same day, before the action started, it was again moved up and put in at another point.)

  (b) *III Army Corps.* (Von Lochow.)

    5th Infantry Division (VREGNY — CELLES 8290—Pt. 169).

      5th Field Artillery Brigade :—

        18th Field Artillery Regiment. (3 field gun and 3 light field howitzer batteries.)

        54th Field Artillery Regiment. (6 field gun batteries.)

6th Infantry Division (AIZY 8693—LA ROYERE FME 8895).
> 6th Field Artillery Brigade :—
>> 3rd Field Artillery Regiment. (6 field gun batteries.)
>> 39th Field Artillery Regiment. (3 field gun, 3 light howitzer batteries.)

Corps Artillery.
> I Battalion, 2nd Guard Foot Artillery Regiment. (4 heavy field howitzer batteries. On 13 Sep., the battalion had been allotted to the 5th Infantry Division, by which it was placed under the 5th Field Artillery Brigade. During the night of 13/14 Sep., the battalion staff and 3 batteries were transferred to the 6th Infantry Division, where they came under the orders of the 6th Field Artillery Brigade. One battery remained with the 5th Infantry Division.)
> Allotted to the Corps. II/45th Field Artillery Regiment (34th Infantry Brigade at JOUY 8494). (3 field gun batteries. The II/45th Field Artillery Regiment belonged to the von Kraewel Detachment formed during the battle of the MARNE from portions of the IX Corps. It fought during the battle with the 34th Infantry Brigade of the IX Corps.)

(c) *VII Reserve Corps.* (Von Zwehl.) (Arrived CHEMIN DES DAMES about 11.30 hours, 13th September.)
> 13th Reserve Division.
>> 13th Reserve Field Artillery Regiment. (6 field gun batteries.)
> 14th Reserve Division.
>> 14th Reserve Field Artillery Regiment. (6 field gun batteries.)
> Corps Artillery.
>> ½ II Battalion, Reserve Foot Artillery Regiment. (2 heavy field howitzer batteries. During the period under consideration the half battalion was attached to the 13th Reserve Division.)

(d) *Attached Army Artillery.*
> III Battalion 4th Foot Artillery Regiment. (Two 21-cm. mortar batteries. During the night of 13/14 Sep., the battalion took up its position and was attached to the 14th Reserve Division.)

9th Cavalry Division.
> 10th Horse Artillery Group. (3 field gun batteries. During the period under consideration the group was attached to the 14th Reserve Division.)

NOTE.—GERMAN Field Artillery Regiments consisted of two Groups (ABTEILUNG) each of 3 batteries. Groups are shown above with ROMAN NUMERALS—*i.e.*, II/45th Field Artillery Regiment.

IX

LEGEND.—FOR USE WITH TRACING OF DISPOSITIONS OF BRITISH AND GERMAN ARTILLERY, 14TH SEPTEMBER, 1914.

German Batteries.	British Batteries.
7·7-cm. Horse Artillery Battery (6 guns).	13-pdr. Battery (6 guns).
7·7-cm. Field Battery (6 guns).	18-pdr. Battery (6 guns).
10·5-cm. Light Field Howitzer Battery (6 guns).	4·5-in. Howitzer Battery (6 guns).
10-cm. Gun Battery (4 guns).	60-pdr. Battery (4 guns).
15-cm. Heavy Field Howitzer Battery (4 guns).	—
21-cm. Mortar Battery (4 guns).	—

German Regiments shown FAR. RES. 13 = 13th Reserve Field Artillery Regiment, or II/17 = II Group of 17th Field Artillery Regiment.

NOTES REGARDING CERTAIN GERMAN UNITS.

A. ½ II Battalion 9th Reserve Foot Artillery Regiment from 10.30 hours until the afternoon—did not come into action.

B. I Battalion 15th Foot Artillery Regiment.

C. II Battalion 4th Foot Artillery Regiment. (Came into action during the night 13th/14th September. Army artillery attached II Corps.)

D. 1st and 3rd Batteries 54th Field Artillery Regiment. In readiness until 1400 hours.

E. 2nd Guard Foot Artillery Regiment.

F. No. 1 Battery, 10th Horse Artillery Group, towards evening and 2nd and 3rd Batteries, 13th Reserve Field Artillery Regiment from 2115 hours.

G. III Battalion 4th Foot Artillery Regiment (21-cm. mortars).

H. 1st Battery and 3/4 of No. 2 Battery, 10th Horse Artillery Group. In readiness.

I. 2nd Battery of 14th Reserve Field Artillery Regiment, from 0830 hours.

K. 5th and 6th Batteries of 14th Reserve Field Artillery Regiment from 1500 hours.

L. First positions of 4th. 5th and 6th Batteries of 14th Reserve Field Artillery Regiment. (No. 4 Battery silenced about 1300 hours.)

M. I Group 14th Reserve Field Artillery Regiment. Forced to cease fire towards 0800 hours.

N. 1 gun, 2nd Battery, 10th Horse Artillery Group.

O. 3rd Battery, 10th Horse Artillery Group.

Q. Second position of 5th Battery, 3rd Field Artillery Regiment.

R. Second position of 5th Battery, 39th Field Artillery Regiment.

S. Second position I Group of 13th Reserve Field Artillery Regiment.

T. 1st Battery of 2nd Guard Foot Artillery Regiment.

U. 2nd Battery of 14th Reserve Field Artillery Regiment, in readiness from 1000 hours.

X. 2nd Reserve Foot Artillery Regiment.

Y. 4th and 5th Batteries, 54th Field Artillery Regiment, from 1530 hours.

Z. Various positions of the six batteries of 18th Field Artillery Regiment.

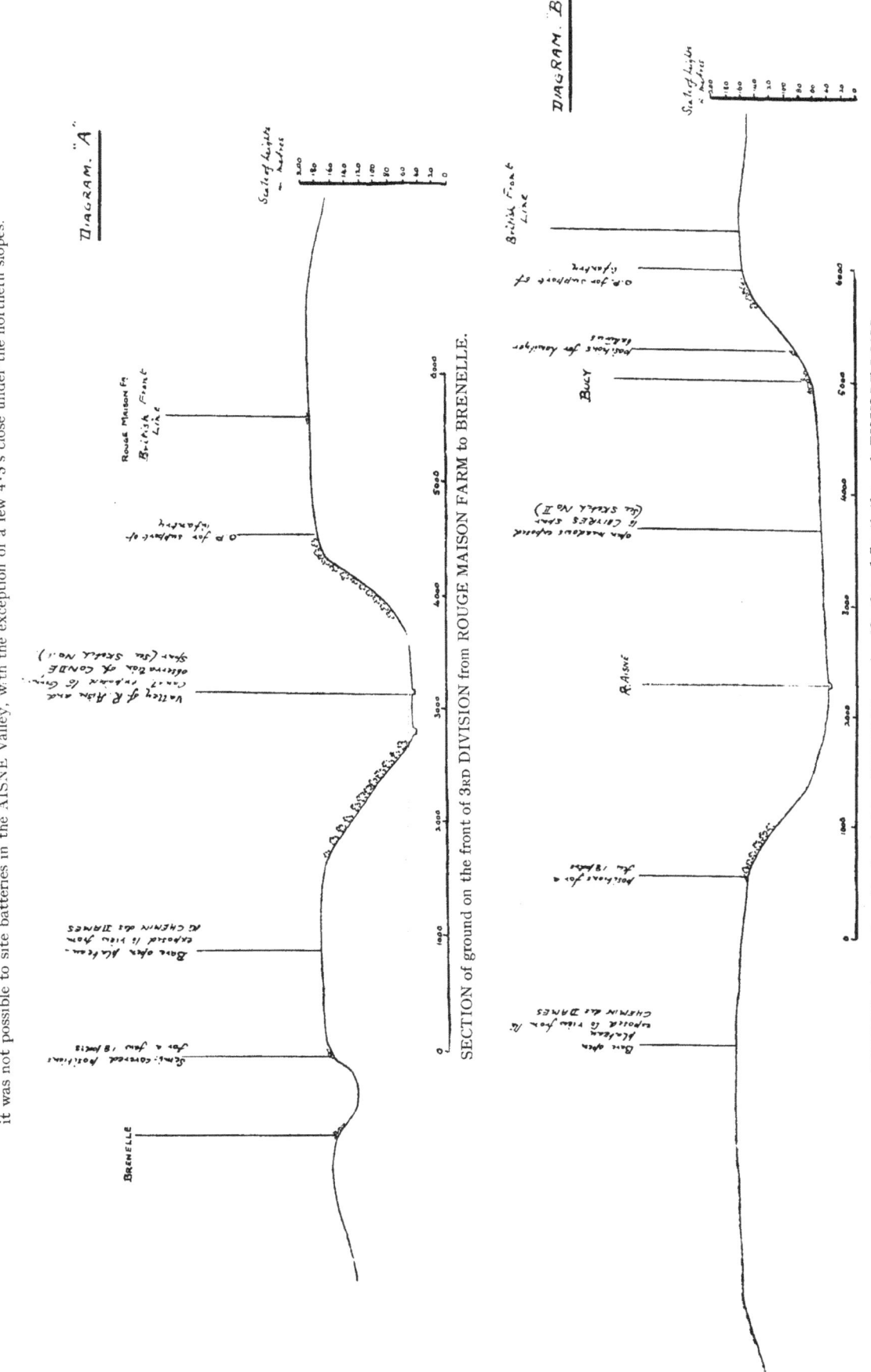

SKETCH No. 5.

PANORAMA from spur North of CONDE about S15900, looking East.
Showing crossings used by 3RD DIVISION and German observation of AISNE Valley.

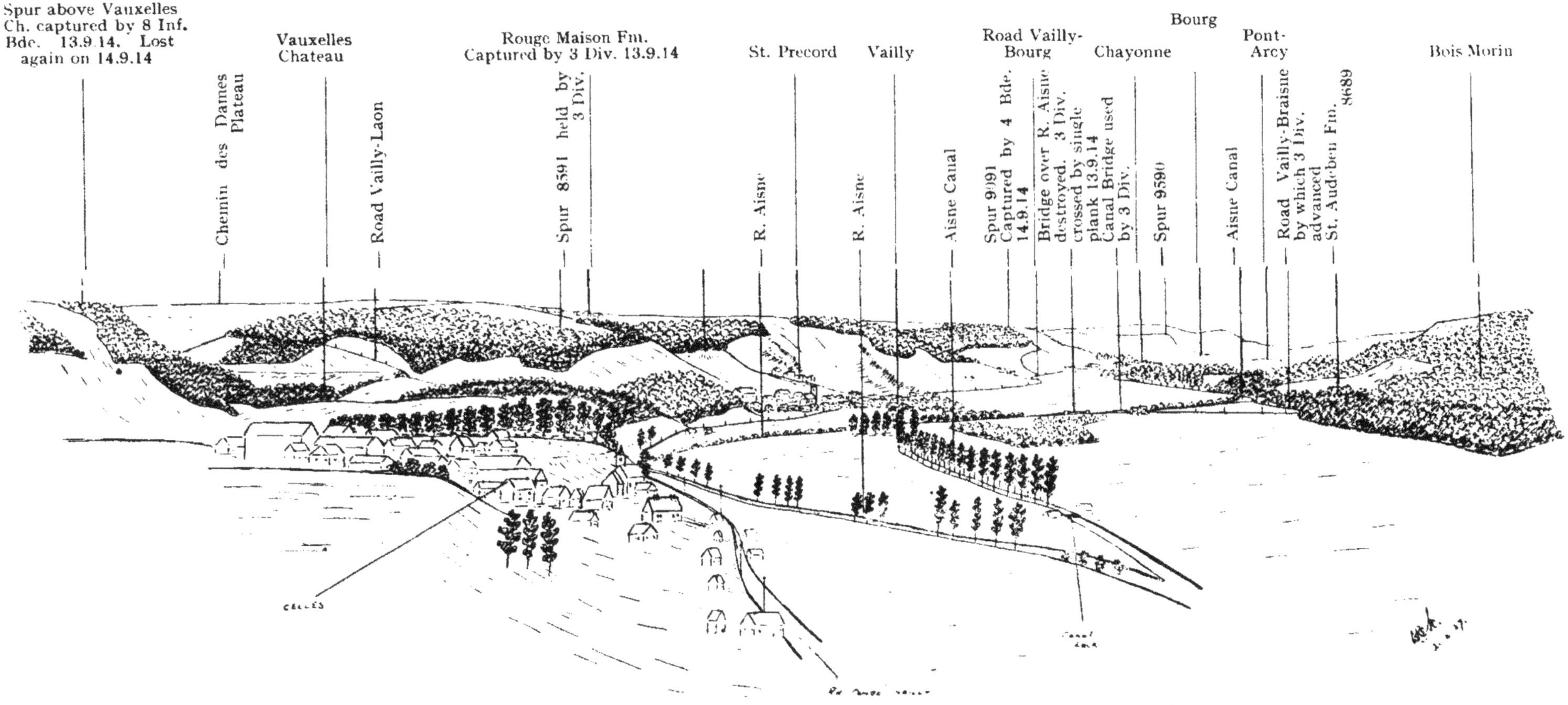

Labels (left to right):

- Spur above Vauxelles Ch. captured by 8 Inf. Bde. 13.9.14. Lost again on 14.9.14
- Chemin des Dames Plateau
- Vauxelles Chateau
- Road Vailly-Laon
- Rouge Maison Fm. Captured by 3 Div. 13.9.14
- Spur 8591 held by 3 Div.
- St. Precord
- R. Aisne
- Vailly
- R. Aisne
- Aisne Canal
- Spur 9091 Captured by 4 Bde.
- Road Vailly-Bourg. Bridge over R. Aisne destroyed. 14.9.14 crossed by single plank 13.9.14
- Chayonne. Canal Bridge used by 3 Div.
- Spur 9590
- Bourg
- Aisne Canal
- Pont-Arcy
- Road Vailly-Braisne by which 3 Div. advanced
- St. Audebrn Fm. 8689
- Bois Morin

SKETCH No. 6.

PANORAMA from CHIVRES SPUR about 80/2886, looking South-west.

Showing crossings used by 4TH and 5TH DIVISIONS and German observation of the AISNE Valley.

Labels (right to left across the panorama):
- Richebourg Spur. Captured by 4 Div. night 12th/13th Sept. 1914
- Pasly Spur
- Road to Chivres
- Bucy-le-Long
- St. Marguerite
- Soissons
- Wood and swampy thickets 7988
- Hill South of Villeneuve St. Germain 7487
- Road Venizel-Bucy
- Open meadows over which Div. advanced
- Chateau de Bellevue
- Wood along R. Aisne 7687
- Road Missy-St. Marguerite
- R. Aisne
- Venizel
- Partially destroyed bridge used by 4 Div.
- Billy sur Aisne
- Sugar Factory
- Bridge at Moulin des Roches constructed by 5 Div.

SKETCH MAP and PANORAMA to illustrate the attack of the 1st DIVISION on TROYON, 14th September, 1914. SKETCH No. 7.
Panorama drawn from 962917 looking North.

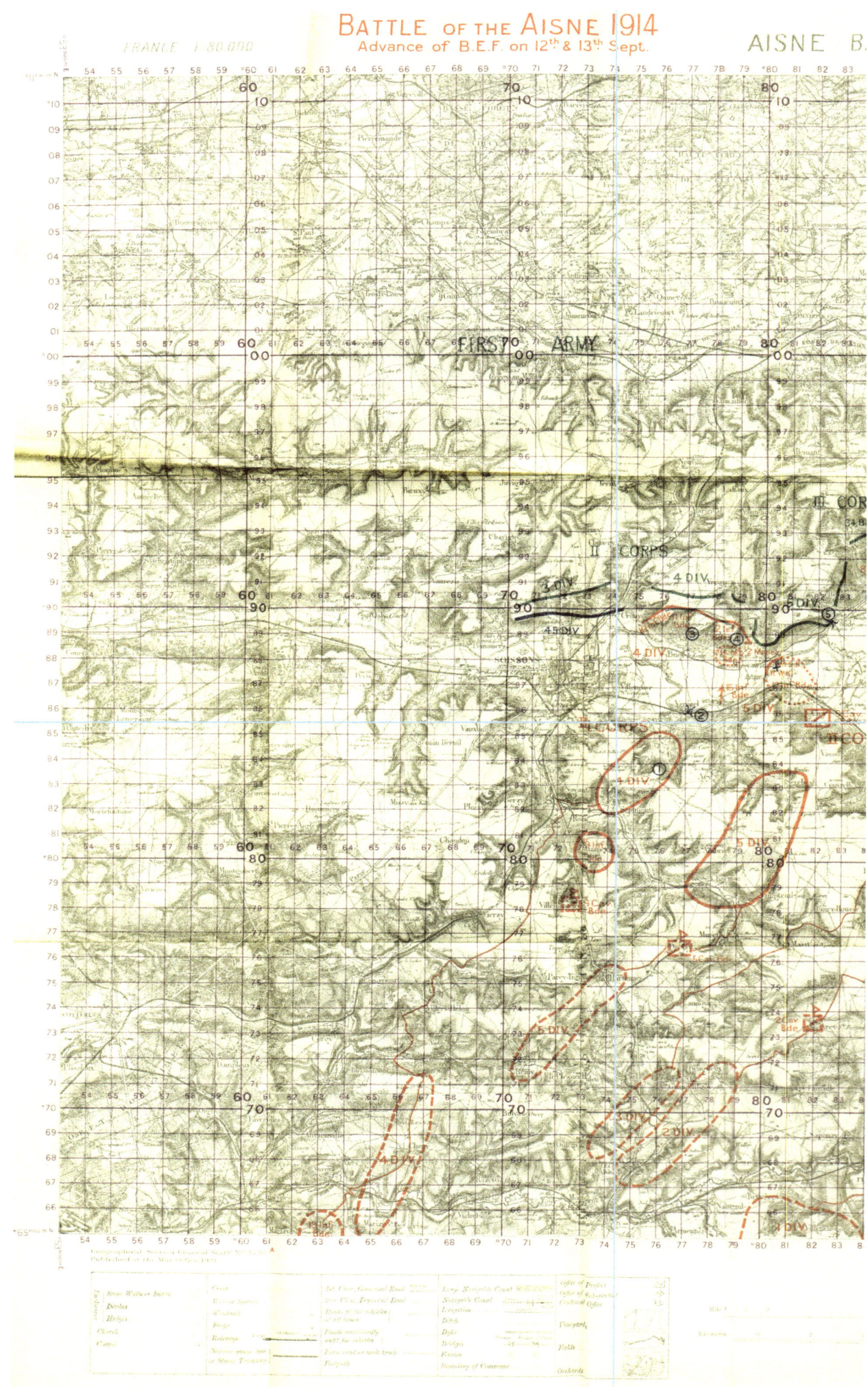

Battle of the Aisne 1914
Advance of B.E.F. on 12th & 13th Sept.

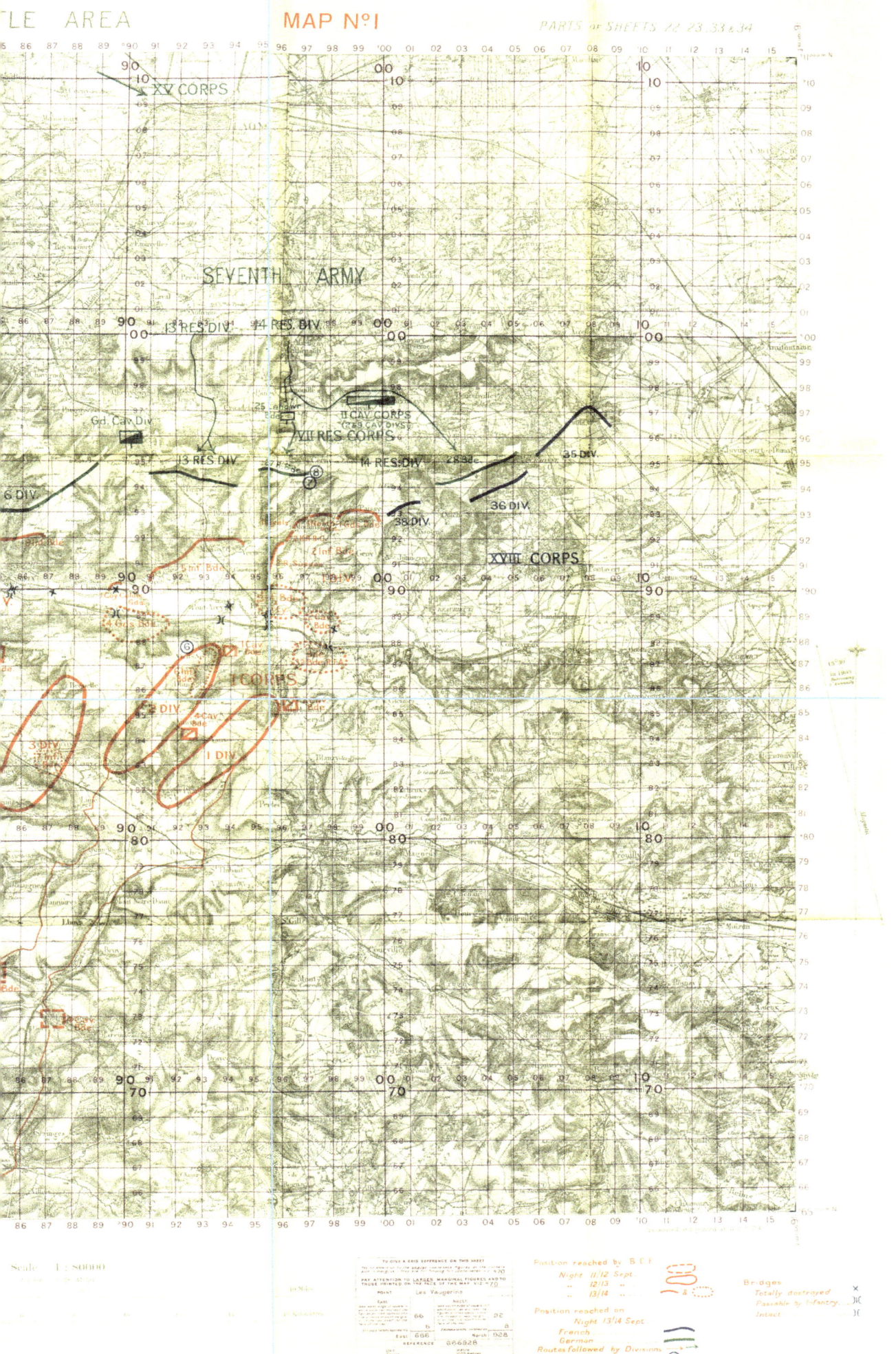

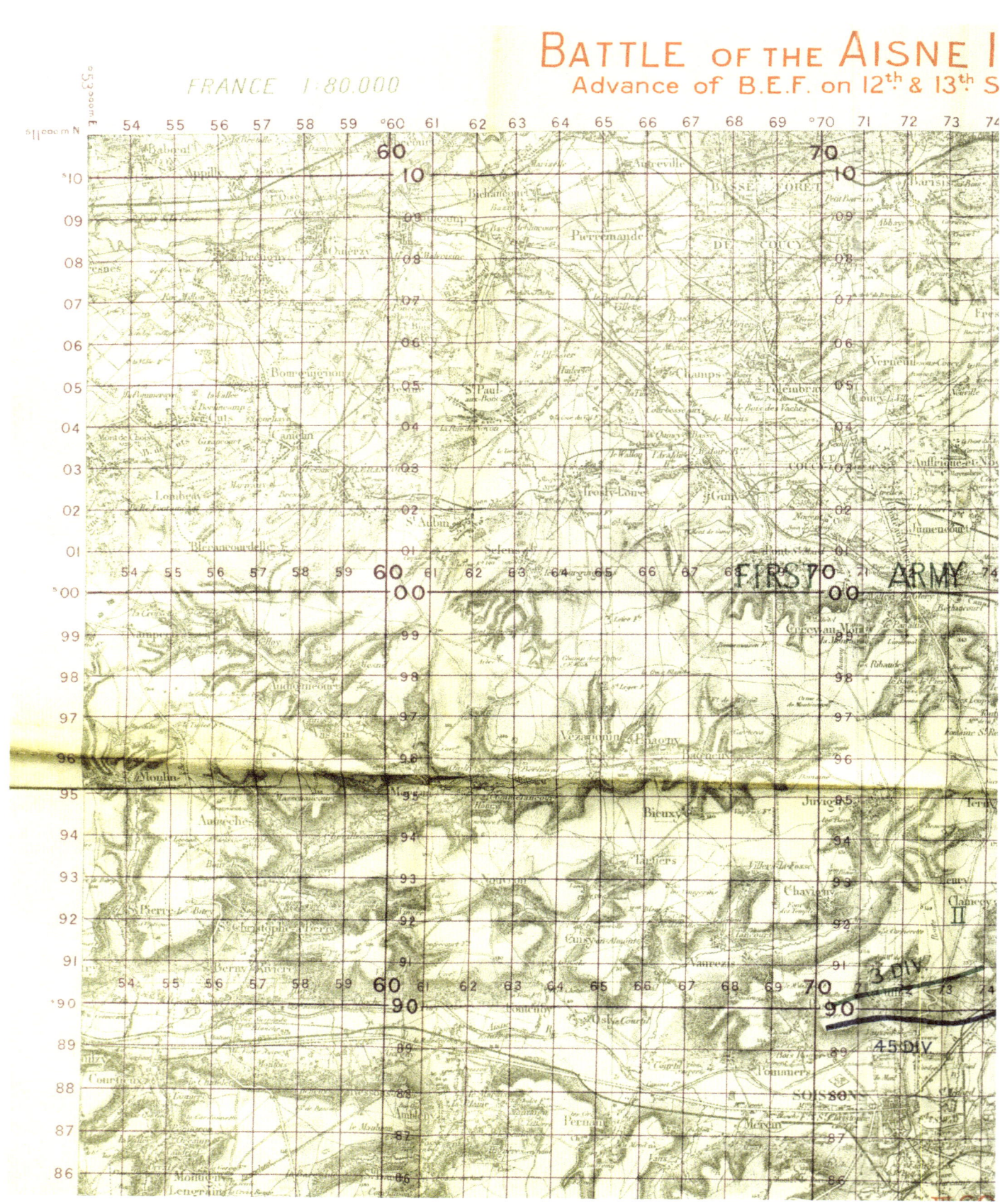

Battle of the Aisne I
Advance of B.E.F. on 12th & 13th S

FRANCE 1:80,000

1914
Sept.

AISNE BATTLE AREA

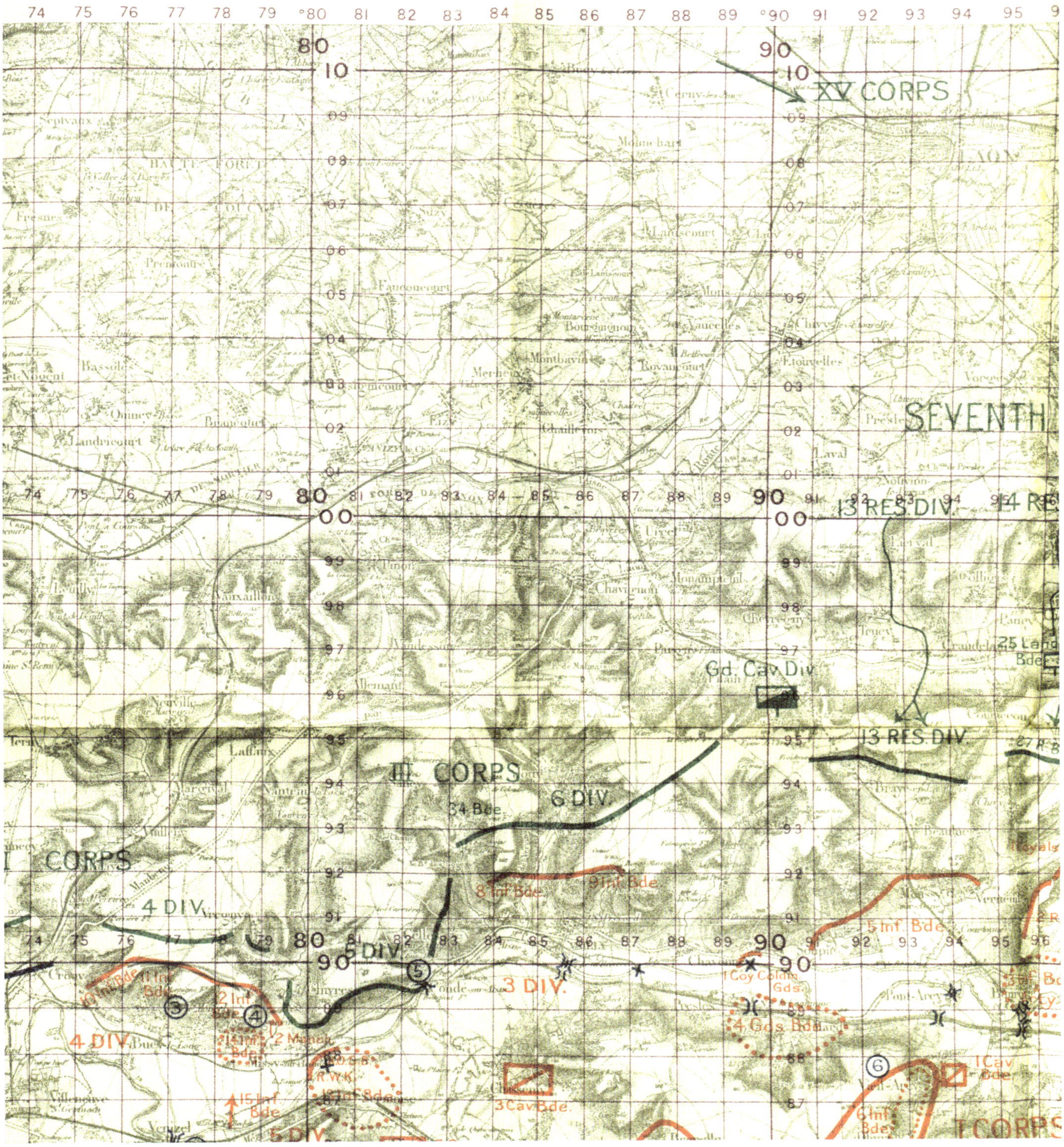

XV CORPS

SEVENTH

13 RES. DIV.

Gd. Cav. Div

13 RES. DIV.

III. CORPS
34 Bde. 6 DIV.

CORPS
4 DIV
8 Inf Bde 9 Inf Bde
5 Inf Bde
5 DIV
3 DIV
1 Coy Colm Gds
3 Inf Bde
2 Manch 4 Gds Bde
4 DIV
R.W.K.
87 Inf Bde
15 Inf Bde
3 Cav Bde
1 Cav Bde
6 Inf Bde
I CORPS

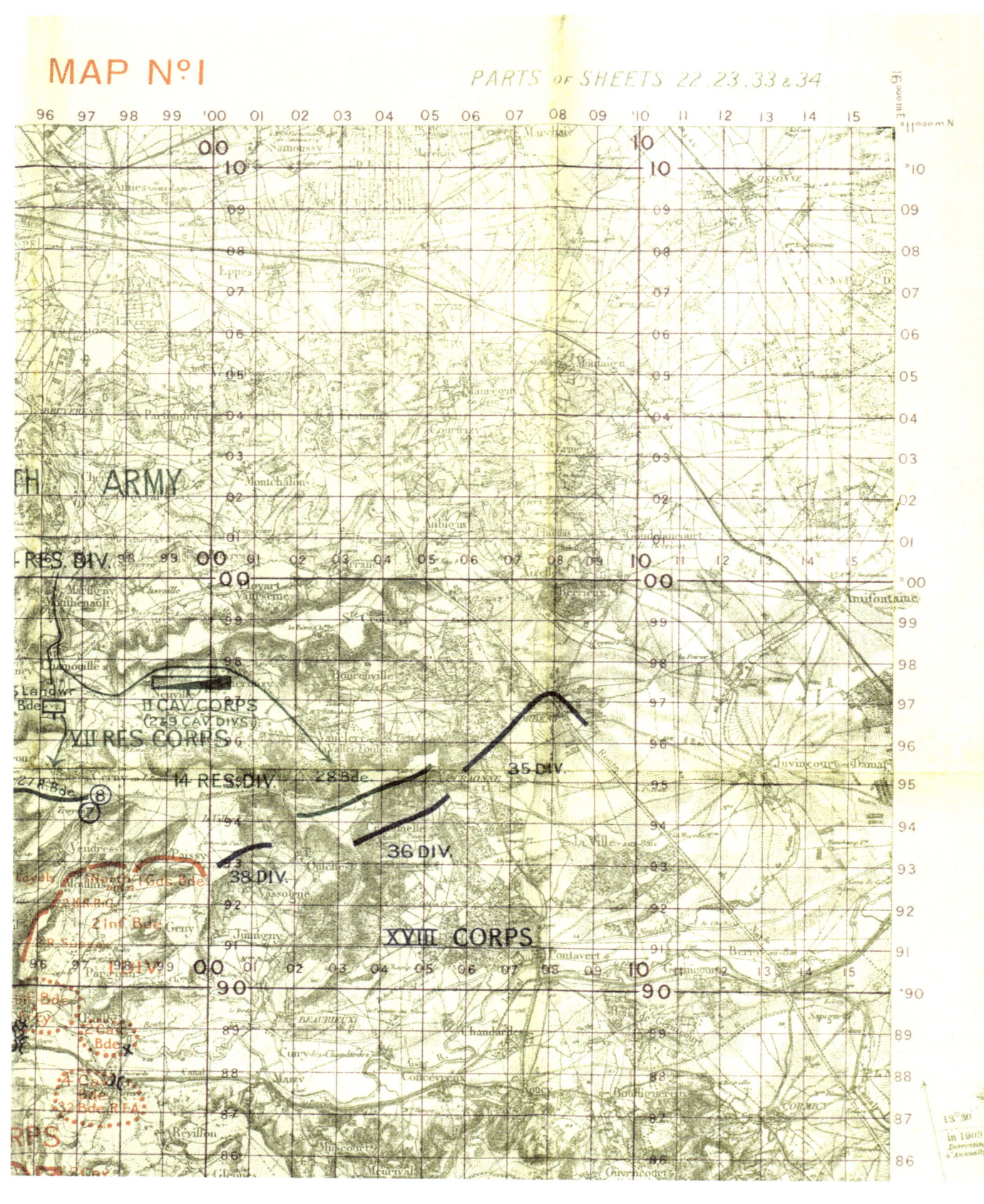

MAP Nº I   PARTS OF SHEETS 22, 23, 33 & 34

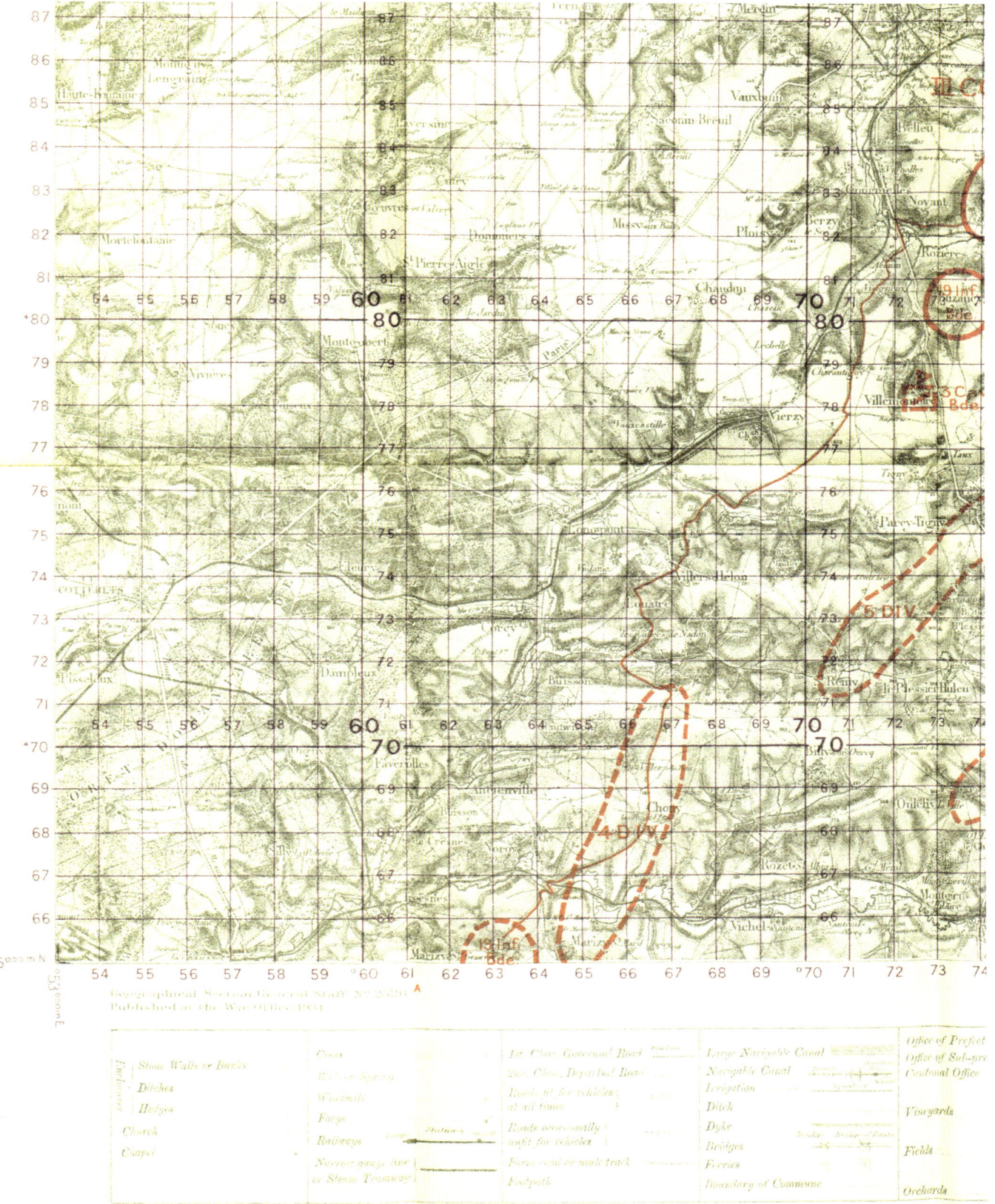

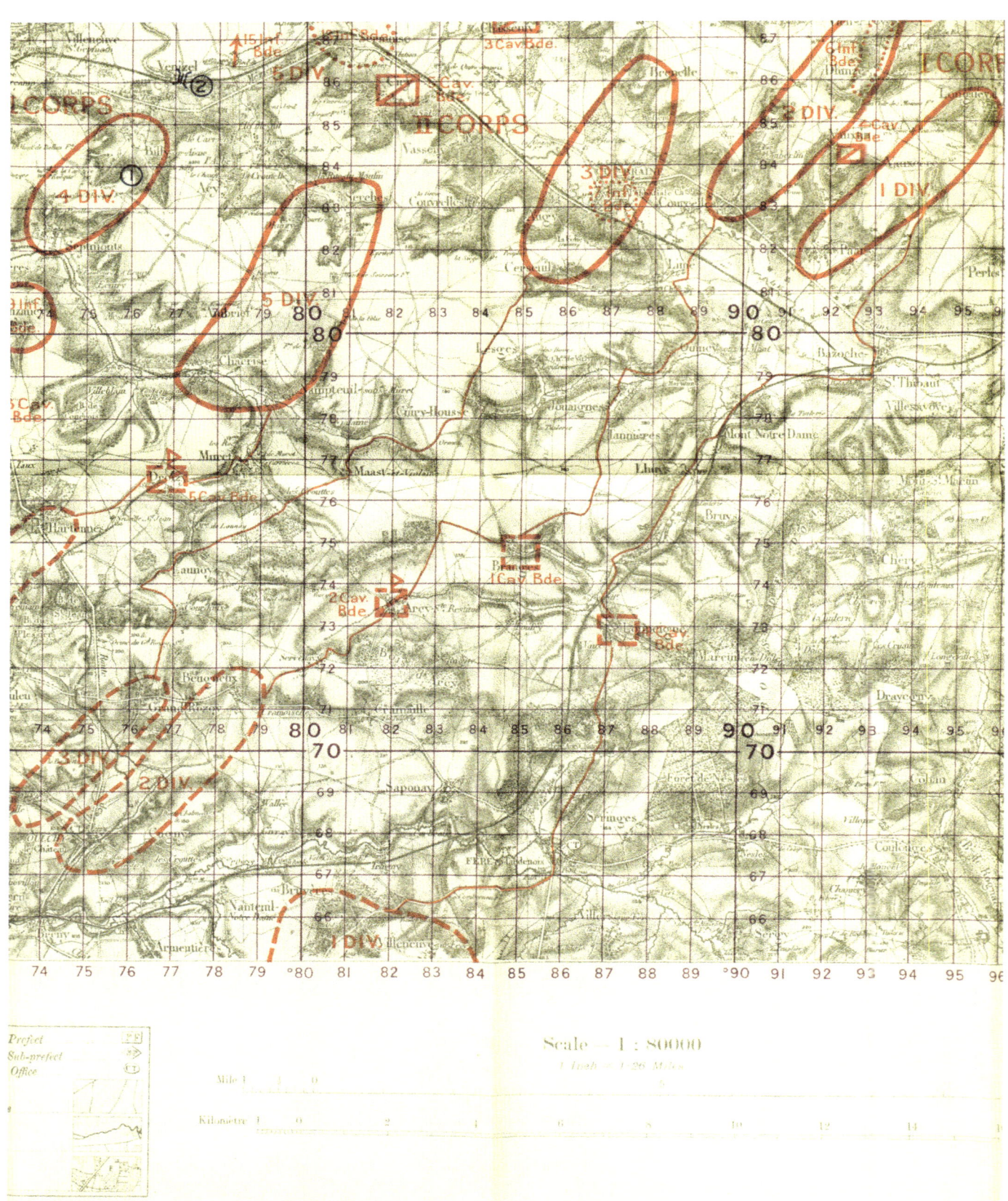

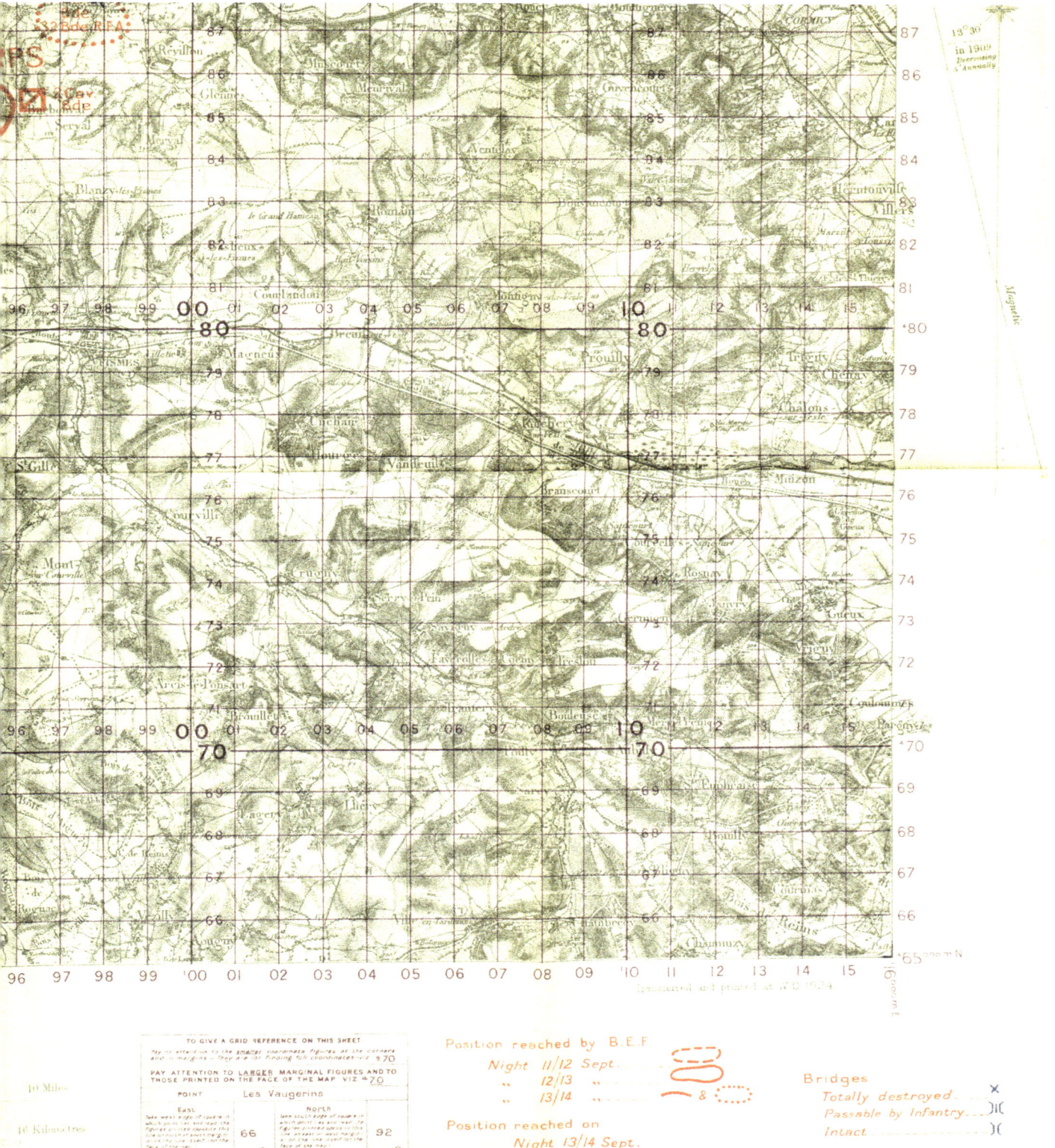

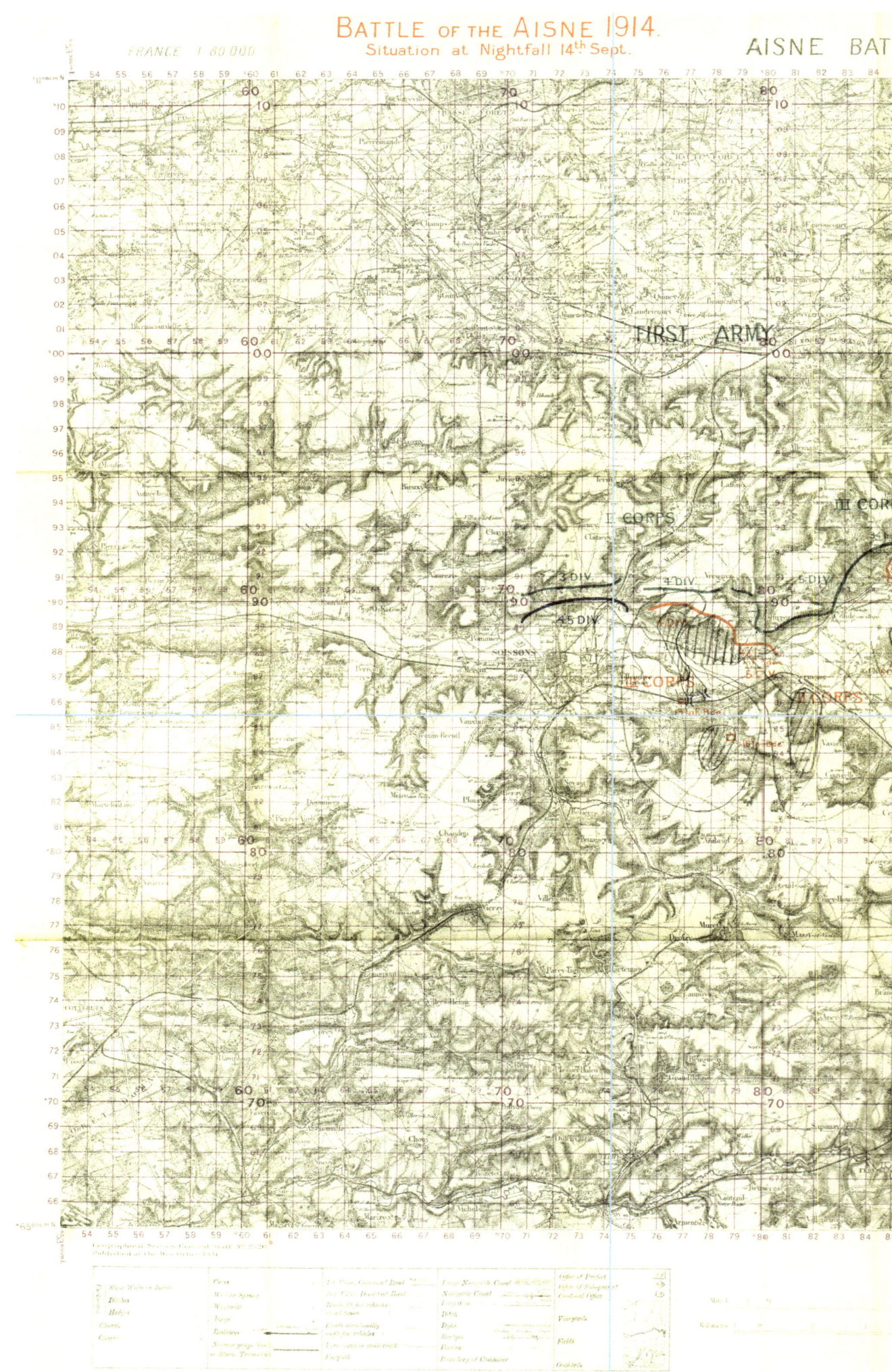

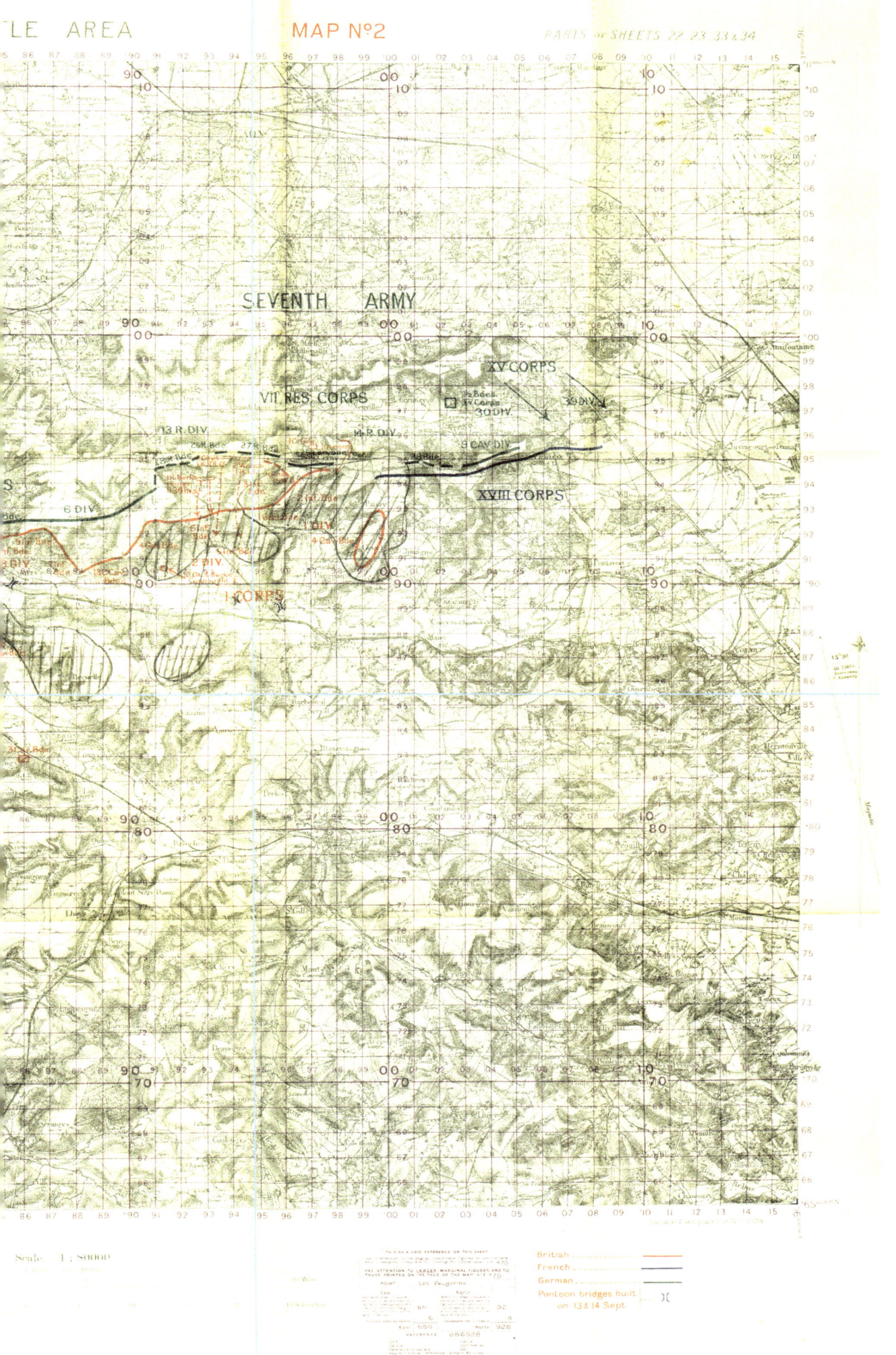

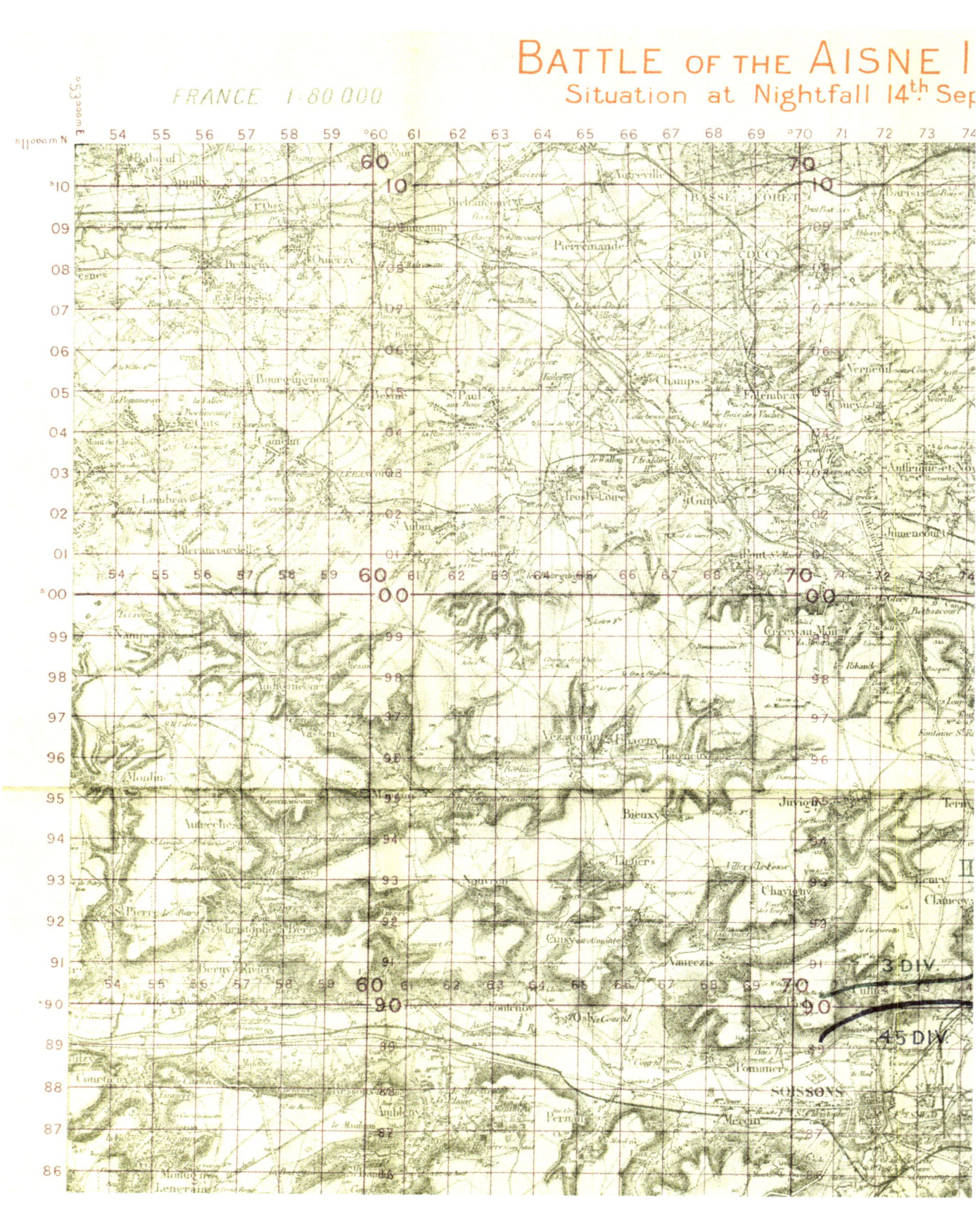

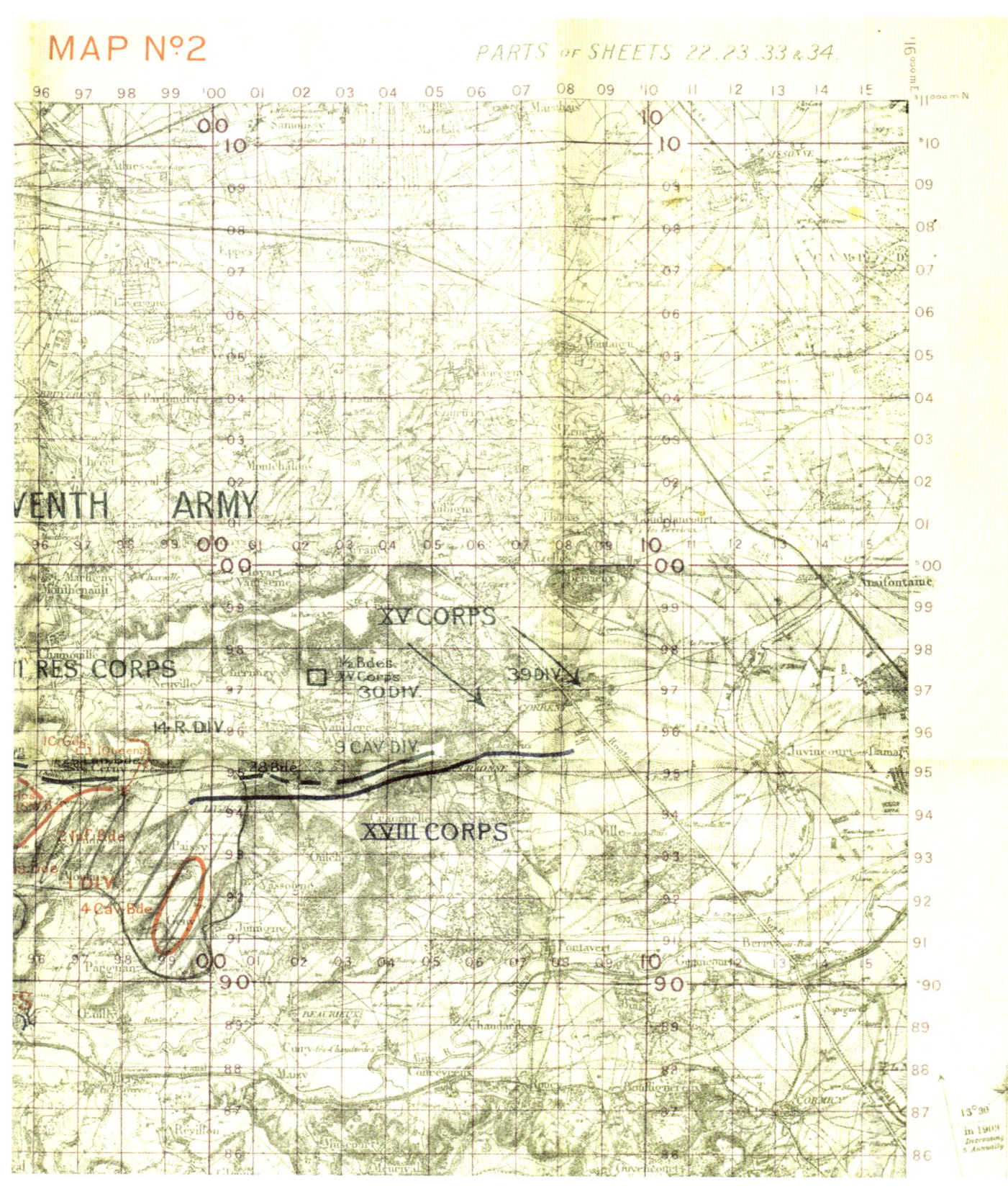

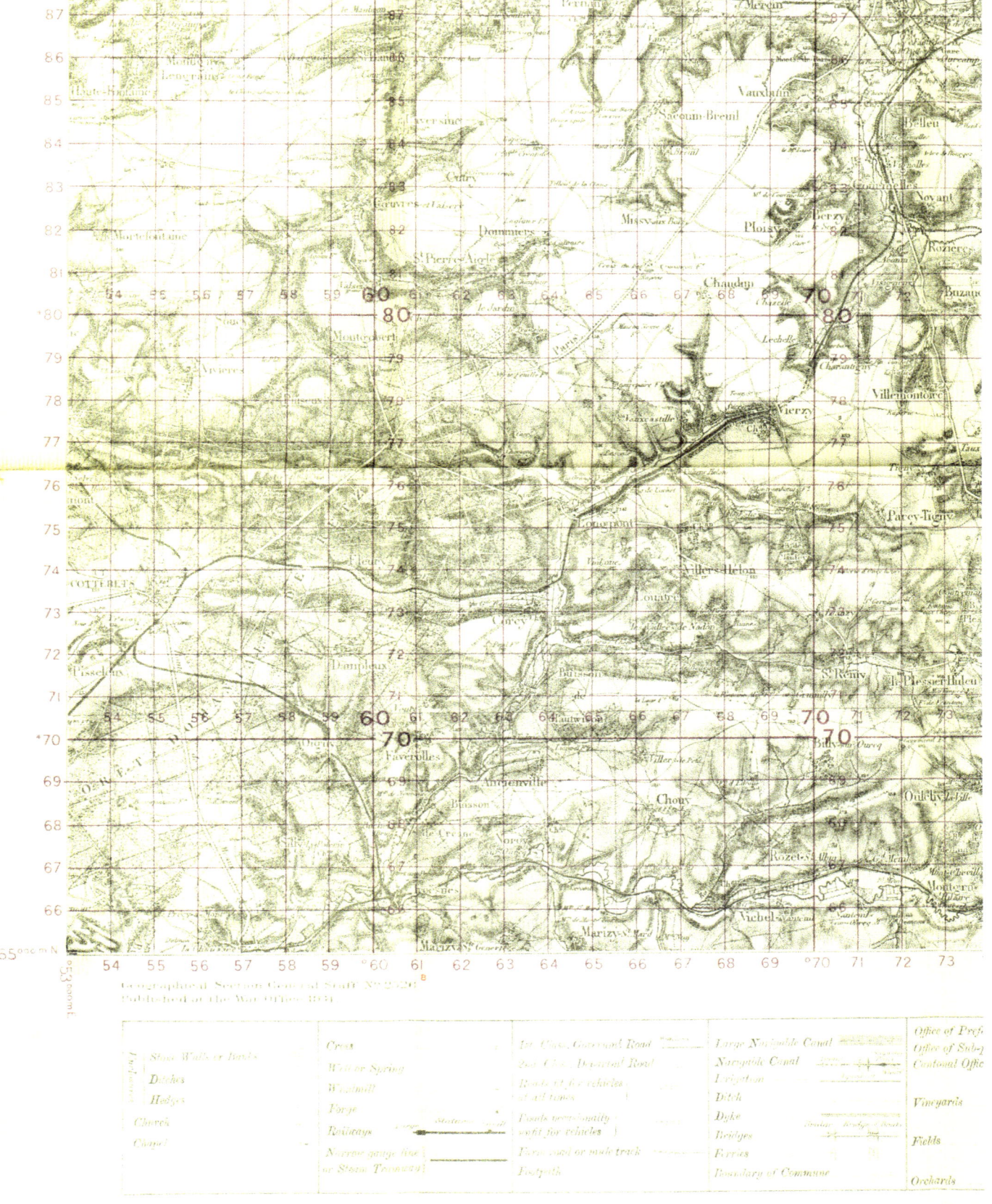

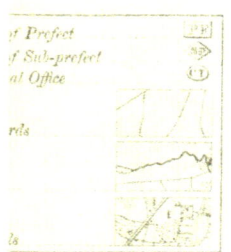

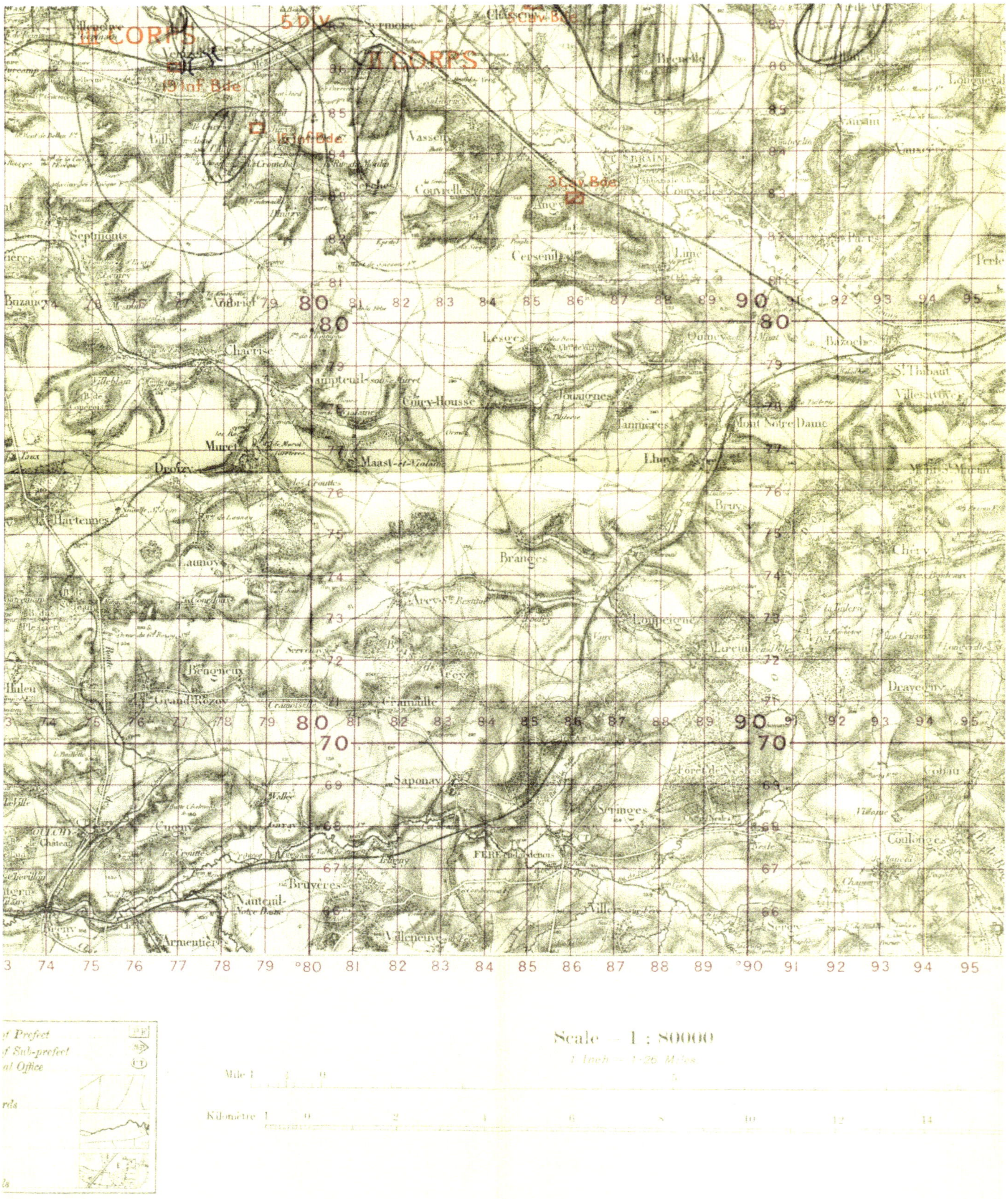

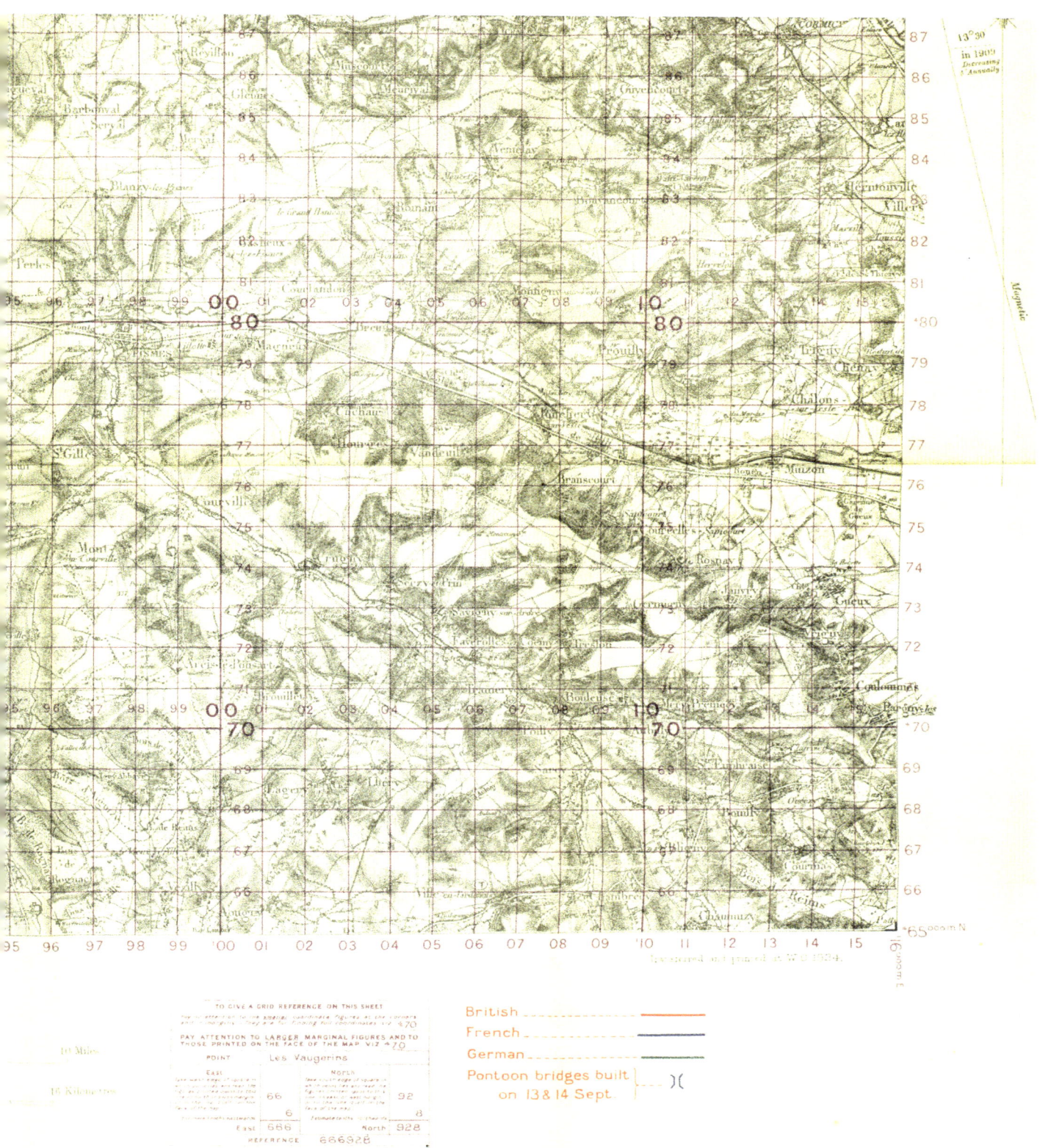

N° 8.

DISPOSITIONS OF THE BRITISH AND GERMAN ARTILLERY.
14TH September 1914

To fit over Map No.2.

War Office 1934

O.R.732.

MAP COMPILED BY
HISTORICAL SECTION, (MILITARY BRANCH)

THE AISNE BATTL

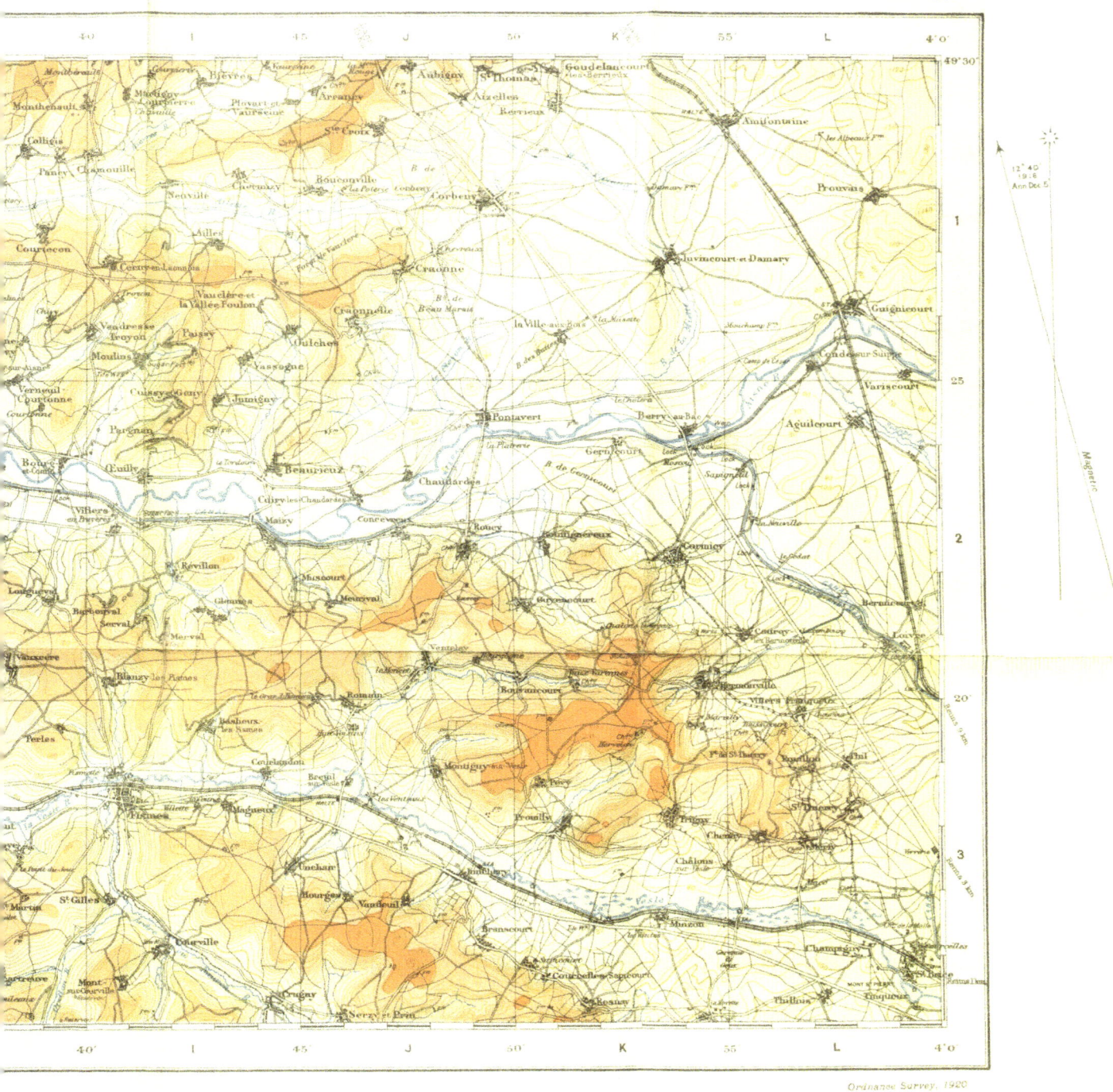

www.ingramcontent.com/pod-product-compliance
Lightning Source LLC
Chambersburg PA
CBHW080903230426
43663CB00014B/2610